Table of Contents

Acknowledgements

5

Vijay, we have journeyed together for 18 wonderful years, filled with countless shared experiences, both joyful and challenging. As a couple, we've not only weathered the ups and downs but have grown stronger through it all.

Here's to many more years of love, laughter, and shared adventures. You're my rock, and I cherish every day we spend together.

To my dearest Amma, Nanna, Sid, Souji, Deepti and Akshara, your love, kindness, and unwavering support have meant the world to me. I hold each of you dearly in my heart. Thank you for being a part of my life.

Preface

Choosing to marry, committing to a serious relationship is a profound decision that shapes the course of one's life. It's a decision influenced by various factors, from physical attraction and astrological compatibility to personal affinities and, of course, love itself.

Yet, in modern life, the path to a successful and enduring partnership has become increasingly complex. Traditionally, the success of a marriage was measured by its ability to fulfil basic physical needs: providing sustenance, clothing, and shelter.

A baseline of kindness and cooperation was deemed sufficient. Husbands and wives often assumed distinct roles within the family structure, contributing to its overall stability.

However, the landscape of love and commitment has evolved, and it now presents a pressing concern—an alarming rise in divorce rates, especially within the first five years of marriage.

Infidelity and emotional disconnection have become distressingly common, challenging the sanctity of this once-revered institution.

The emergence of dating sites and marriage matrimony platforms has reshaped how individuals connect with potential partners, yet the persistent increase in divorce rates signals that something essential is missing. Technology alone cannot bridge the gap.

The empowerment of women, smaller family sizes, ambitious career pursuits, and changing family structures are further redefining relationships.

Moreover, the scars of childhood, marked by parent's quarrels, abuse, or suppression, can lead to a profound fear of commitment.

These experiences shape perceptions of relationships and commitment, often leading to hesitations about entering into committed partnerships. Some are even questioning the institution of marriage itself, influenced by a global shift towards alternative living arrangements.

In this evolving landscape, it becomes even more crucial for individuals to understand what comprises a happy and healthy partnership. Emotional connection, mutual support, and compatibility are paramount in modern unions.

 Yet, many find themselves ill-equipped or inadequately informed about the intricate dynamics involved in sustaining a healthy, enduring relationship or embarking on a committed, long-lasting partnership.

Within these pages, my aim is to guide you through the multifaceted elements essential for nurturing emotional intimacy and compatibility in modern relationships.
I take into account the ever-changing dynamics of contemporary society, acknowledge the role of

independence, and understand the complexities of those who may not initially seek commitment.

I delve into the evolving intricacies of relationships, providing insights for individuals at various stages of their romantic journey.

Whether you're exploring the possibility of long-term relationships, embarking on the path to marriage, navigating the early stages of newlywed life, or seeking to rekindle the emotional connection in your partnership, this book is tailored to your needs.

Throughout this journey, I will serve as your guide, skilfully laying the foundation for a robust and enduring marriage or committed partnership that thrives on love, compatibility, and happiness.

Chapter 1: Establishing the Foundation

Stages of Marriage

Marriage is a journey that unfolds through various stages, each offering its unique set of experiences and challenges. Understanding and navigating these stages can significantly contribute to the strength and longevity of a marital bond.

The **_honeymoon_** stage marks the early days of marriage, characterized by deep infatuation and emotional connection. During this period, couples are often deeply in love and eager to explore every facet of their partner's personality.

Open and meaningful communication is vital during this phase, allowing partners to build a strong emotional connection and establish trust. Learning about each other's dreams, aspirations, and quirks lays the foundation for a deeper understanding as the relationship matures.

As the relationship progresses into the **_adjustment and_**

realization stage, couples begin to encounter differences and challenges.

This stage is a natural part of any relationship as partners adapt to living together and sharing their lives. The key is how couples navigate these challenges. Taking the time to understand each other's needs, expectations, and communication styles leads to more effective problem-solving and conflict resolution.

Couples who invest in their relationship during these early stages develop a strong sense of intimacy, trust, and mutual support.

The ***parenthood*** stage often follows, marked by the arrival of children. While bringing children into the family can be a joyous and fulfilling experience, it also introduces new complexities. Parents must learn to balance their roles as partners and caregivers. Effective communication and teamwork are essential in this stage as couples face the challenges and joys of raising a family together.

Later in marriage, the ***empty nest*** stage may emerge as children grow and leave home. This stage presents an opportunity for couples to reconnect and rediscover each other. It's a time to focus on personal growth, shared interests, and the evolving dynamics of the relationship.

Finally, the ***golden years*** stage is a reflection of a lifetime together. Couples in this stage have weathered life's storms, celebrated successes, and grown together. It's a time to cherish the memories created throughout the journey and to continue nurturing the love and companionship that have sustained the marriage.

In essence, marriage is a journey through these stages, each offering valuable lessons and opportunities for growth. Couples who actively invest in their relationship, communicate openly, and adapt to changing circumstances are more likely to build a lasting and fulfilling partnership.

The stages of marriage provide a roadmap for couples to navigate life's challenges and celebrate its joys together.

Foundations of marriage

The Foundation of Friendship

One of the most fundamental aspects that form a healthy and enduring marriage is the strength and quality of the friendship between partners. When couples are not just life partners but also best friends, their relationship flourishes. Friendship fosters comfort, companionship, and a sense of fun that we all cherish. In a strong friendship, couples have each other's backs and strive not to hurt one another intentionally. Just as we avoid causing pain to our dearest friends, couples who value their friendship with the same sensitivity create marriages that are sanctuaries of trust and support.

Unity as a Single Unit

After marriage, couples often face external influences, particularly from their families. While family support is essential, it's crucial for couples to act as a single unit when making decisions. This means presenting a united front and working together to reach agreements.

It's common for couples to seek advice from their parents, but it's equally important to ensure that these conversations do not undermine the unity of the partnership. Couples should prioritise discussing important matters with each other first, seeking guidance from parents or other trusted sources if necessary.

Balancing Sharing and Privacy

The balance between sharing personal information and maintaining privacy is a delicate one. Couples should discuss their boundaries and comfort levels regarding what they share with others, especially when it comes to sensitive topics or disagreements.

Sharing happy moments with parents can strengthen family bonds and create a supportive network. However, for resolving conflicts or dealing with more personal issues, it may be advisable to seek help from professionals or confide in close friends who can offer an objective perspective.

Parents and their generation may have different beliefs and values. While their advice can be valuable, it may not always align with the couple's unique circumstances and priorities. Couples should consider this when deciding whose guidance to seek and when to rely on their own judgment.

Navigating the Path to Commitment

In a world brimming with options and influenced by countless fairy tales, romantic dramas, and societal expectations, the journey towards commitment in a relationship can be a tumultuous one. It's not uncommon to find yourself grappling with a fear of commitment or holding unrealistic ideals shaped by external influences. In this chapter, we will explore the common challenges that can impede your path to a fulfilling partnership and discover how to overcome them.

The Perfection Paradox

From Cinderella's glass slipper to the dashing heroes of K-dramas, popular culture often presents idealised versions of love and perfection. These portrayals can set unrealistic standards for real-life partnerships.

The fear of commitment may arise when we fixate on finding the "perfect" partner, someone who embodies the looks, charm, and charisma of our on-screen idols. The reality is that perfection is an illusion, and every individual comes with their unique blend of qualities and flaws.

Analysis Paralysis

In an era of endless choices and opportunities, it's easy to become paralysed by the fear of making the wrong decision. You might hesitate to commit because you're constantly searching for the elusive "better" option.

 This fear can lead to a pattern of serial dating without ever settling into a meaningful relationship. Overcoming this hurdle involves recognising that relationships are not about finding the "best" option but about building something meaningful with someone who complements your values and aspirations.

Rushing into Commitment

On the flip side, a fear of prolonged singlehood or societal pressures can sometimes drive individuals to hastily accept the first available option.
This rush into commitment, born out of desperation, can obscure judgment and result in   ill-suited partnerships. Balancing the desire for companionship with a patient and discerning approach to finding the right partner is of utmost importance.

The Unrealistic Checklist

Often, individuals come into relationships with a checklist of qualities they believe their partner must possess. This checklist can be influenced by cultural norms, materialistic desires, or the pursuit of an idealised lifestyle.

 While shared values and some common interests are vital, harbouring an extensive checklist can hinder your ability to build a meaningful connection. Prioritising essential qualities over superficial ones is a crucial step towards overcoming the fear of commitment.

Managing Expectations

Lastly, managing your expectations is key to a successful and committed relationship. It's essential to understand that no partnership is devoid of challenges. The early stages of a relationship are often marked by infatuation and excitement, but as time progresses, you'll encounter differences and disagreements.

It's important to approach relationships with a realistic mindset, understanding that no one person can fulfil all your needs or desires. Compromise, communication, and collaboration are the cornerstones of a strong commitment.

Transition to the Next Chapter

Now that we've explored the various challenges and fears that can shape our approach to commitment, it's time to delve deeper into the heart of building a strong and lasting relationship – getting to know each other.

In the following chapters, we will navigate the intricate terrain of understanding your partner on a profound level. This journey will involve not only discovering your partner's hopes, dreams, and fears but also sharing your own.

Together, we will unlock the secrets to fostering emotional intimacy and cultivating a connection that stands the test of time. So, let's embark on this voyage of mutual discovery and strengthen the foundation of your relationship.

Chapter 2: Cultivating the Foundation of Love

Love is often described as a complex, intangible feeling, characterized by a sense of chemistry and initial attraction, akin to infatuation. This unexplainable affection can serve as the starting point for a deeper and enduring love.

But what transforms infatuation into lasting, genuine love? When people attempt to define love, they often mention feeling at home with their partner, as if they are seeing themselves in the other person. "Safety" is another commonly used term, signifying comfort in being one's true self and feeling supported in life's journey.

Knowing each other

As you embark on the journey of getting to know someone who could potentially be your life partner, whether it's through a blind date, a marriage proposal, or a meeting facilitated by a matrimony website or dating app, it's essential to go beyond mere physical appearances.

One of the most valuable gifts you can offer yourself and your partner is the opportunity to live in accordance with your core values, beliefs, and true selves.

When you encourage and enable your partner to align their life with their deeply held principles, it brings about a profound sense of fulfilment and completeness.

However, achieving this requires genuine conversations — not just surface - level exchanges, but a willingness to invite each other into your inner worlds. It involves sharing your thoughts, dreams, aspirations, fears, failures, insecurities, and uncertainties.

For a shared life to flourish, you both need to understand what defines and drives each other. This level of sharing creates a deep connection and understanding between partners, fostering a sense of closeness that superficial interactions alone cannot achieve.

Admittedly, it can be intimidating to reveal so much about yourself to someone you've just met. You might wonder if you're creating the right impression or question whether it's too soon to share your deeper thoughts. However, it's crucial to show your authentic self right from the beginning.

If you're not comfortable letting others see the real you, how can you envision a future together with someone who cannot accept you for who you are?

By allowing each other into your innermost selves, you become more vulnerable, more human, and it marks the first step towards developing emotional intimacy.

Our inner selves are intricate and multifaceted, and sharing them with a partner is an act of vulnerability that forms the basis of emotional intimacy. Through this vulnerability, you invite your partner into your inner world, sharing your thoughts, dreams, fears, and the inexplicable emotions that make you human.

During this process, observe your partner's reactions. Are they treating you with respect? Are they casual when you talk about your aspirations, dreams, or ambitions, or are they accepting and non-judgmental?

These observations allow you to quickly assess whether you should continue on this path. When you notice that your partner is treating your inner world with care and reverence, being respectful and non-judgmental, it creates a safe space for both of you to be authentic, encouraging you to open up even further.

Going deeper in understanding each other is the first step towards forming a profound emotional connection, which is a signal to continue your journey and explore the next facet: human needs.

To get you started, here are some icebreaker questions that can serve as a foundation for more meaningful conversations. These questions delve into practical aspects of life and deeper emotional connections, helping you better understand your partner's values, experiences, and aspirations. They enable you to make informed decisions about the potential for a fulfilling and compatible long-term relationship.

Knowing Each Other Questions:

1. Tell me something about yourself. Who are your family, what do you do, and what are your hobbies and interests?

2. What are your life goals and aspirations? Discussing long-term life goals allows you to see if your individual life paths are heading in similar directions, helping you assess whether your future plans are compatible.

3. Are you someone who enjoys books or seeks adventure? Discovering your partner's basic personality and interests enables you to support and share in their enthusiasm, creating a stronger bond.

4. How have your relationships shaped you? This includes family, past relationships, and friendships. Understanding these influences provides context for your partner's beliefs and behaviours.

5. What are the things that make you angry? Identifying triggers for anger or frustration helps you navigate potential conflicts and understand each other's boundaries.

6. Do you have spiritual beliefs, and how do they affect your daily life and choices? Spiritual beliefs can be deeply ingrained and influence decision-making. Understanding your partner's beliefs helps you understand their moral compass.

7. What are your culinary preferences? Discussing your daily eating habits, whether vegetarian, non-vegetarian, vegan, or other preferences, helps determine if your food choices align.

8. Can you share a significant milestone that has shaped you? Sharing significant life experiences provides insight into your character, resilience, and the factors that have influenced your perspectives on life.

9. How do you define success? Clarifying what success means to your partner can help you work together toward common goals.

10. What strategies do you employ to uplift yourself when you're feeling down? Learning about the coping mechanisms your partner uses during difficult times enables you to provide comfort and support.

11. What are you most proud of about yourself? Celebrating your partner's achievements and sources of pride fosters positivity and self-esteem within the relationship.

12. How do you perceive your strengths and weaknesses? Self-awareness is crucial for personal growth. Understanding their strengths and weaknesses can help your partner continually improve themselves.

13. What brings you happiness? Exploring the things that bring inner joy reveals what truly fulfils your partner, allowing you to nurture their happiness.

14. Can you describe a typical workday or a perfect day on holiday? Knowing what your partner envisions as a perfect day provides opportunities for creating memorable experiences together.

15. How do you recharge your emotional batteries? Understanding how your partner rejuvenates their emotional well-being allows you to support their self-care practices.

16. What are your views on health, fitness, diet, and sleep? Understanding how your partner perceives health allows you to support and share common goals for your well-being.

17. Living Arrangements:
  - Do you envision living with your parents or in a nuclear family setup after marriage?
  - Have you ever considered the possibility of living abroad for work or other opportunities?
  - Are you open to relocating to different cities or countries for career prospects?

18. Work Preferences:
  - Do you prefer working from home or going to the office every day?
  - Are you inclined towards a stable 9-to-6 job or do you have an interest in freelancing or flexible work arrangements?
  - What are your thoughts on night shifts, and how do you envision managing your work-life balance if you have late evening shifts?

Knowing each other needs

In a healthy and mature relationship, both partners have needs that should be acknowledged and met through mutual effort. When individuals choose to marry, they ideally bring emotional health and maturity to the relationship. It's crucial not to carry unresolved conflicts or the unrealistic expectation that marriage will miraculously fix perceived inadequacies.

It's important to be aware that certain issues, such as violence, alcohol, drug problems, or mental health issues, can create significant emotional demands within a marriage. These challenges can be draining on both partners and should serve as red flags that require immediate attention and resolution.

In a successful partnership, both individuals share the responsibility of expressing their needs and prioritising their partner's needs in a healthy manner. There are various reasons why people may hesitate to state their needs. Some might believe that their partner should intuitively understand their desires (although mind-reading is not a realistic expectation).

Others may view expressing their needs as a sign of weakness or selfishness. Some individuals may not have a clear understanding of their own needs, while others might feel that it's too much effort to ask, fearing that their partner won't listen or respond positively.

Whether in a marriage, friendship, workplace relationship, or business partnership, relationships thrive when both parties needs are met. The success of any relationship can be measured by how well each person's needs are served.

This requires a delicate balance where both individuals contribute to the well-being of the other and the relationship itself. It's essential to avoid becoming overly dependent on one another, as excessive neediness can drain the partner and weaken the relationship.

In an ideal scenario, acts of love and kindness are carried out sincerely, not as transactions with an expectation of receiving something in return.

A mindset of "I do for you, you do for me" can be destructive. Instead, both partners should act out of genuine care and love. When kindness is received from a partner, it should be met with gratitude rather than taken for granted.

In summary, a successful and fulfilling relationship is built on the foundation of understanding, respecting, and meeting each other's needs while maintaining a healthy balance. Both partners should contribute to the relationship's well-being without keeping score or expecting something in return for their efforts.

Understanding and addressing each other's needs is vital for a healthy and fulfilling relationship. Here are some examples of how partners can satisfy each other's needs:

1. **The need to feel loved**: Express love through verbal affirmations, physical affection, and spending quality time

together. Surprise your partner with acts of kindness and thoughtfulness.

2. **The need to feel valued**: Show appreciation for your partner's efforts and accomplishments. Acknowledge their contributions to the relationship and express gratitude.

3. **The need to be respected**: Listen actively to your partner's opinions and ideas, even when you disagree. Avoid belittling or criticizing them and treat their feelings and boundaries with respect.

4. **The need to feel special or unique**: Celebrate your partner's individuality and uniqueness. Compliment their distinctive qualities and express admiration for what sets them apart.

5. **The need to be appreciated**: Acknowledge and thank your partner for the little things they do. Express gratitude for their support, whether it's emotional or practical.

6. **The need to be admired**: Recognise your partner's strengths and accomplishments. Share your admiration for their abilities and achievements.

7. **The need to express love physically and sexually**: Prioritise physical intimacy in the relationship. Communicate openly about your desires and explore each other's preferences.

8. **The need to feel cared for:** Show concern for your partner's well-being. Check in on their emotional state and offer comfort and support during challenging times.

9. **The need to feel that you are a priority:** Make an effort to spend quality time together and prioritize your partner's needs and feelings in your daily life.

10. **The need to feel safe**: Create a safe and secure environment where your partner feels comfortable sharing their thoughts, fears, and vulnerabilities. Be a source of emotional support.

11. **The need to spend time together:** Plan activities and outings that you both enjoy. Allocate time in your schedule for shared experiences and quality bonding.

12. **The need to spend time alone**: Respect your partner's need for personal space and independence. Allow them time for hobbies, self-reflection, or relaxation without feeling neglected.

13. **The need to have fun**: Inject fun and excitement into your relationship by trying new activities, sharing laughter, and enjoying playful moments together.

14. **The need to relate to others, socialise:** Encourage your partner to maintain connections with friends and family. Support their social life and participate in social activities together.

15. **The need to pursue a professional life:** Be supportive of your partner's career goals and ambitions. Offer encouragement and understanding during work-related challenges.

16. **The need to have financial safety**: Collaborate on financial planning and budgeting. Discuss long-term financial goals and work together to achieve them.

17. **The need to be intellectually stimulated:** Engage in meaningful conversations and share your thoughts and ideas. Explore mutual interests and encourage intellectual growth.

18. **The need to converse**: Foster open and honest communication. Create an atmosphere where both partners can express themselves without fear of judgment.

19. **The need to be honest and expect honesty**: Build trust through transparency and open communication. Honesty is the foundation of a healthy relationship.

20. **The need to create a family**: Discuss your family goals and aspirations. Plan for the future and support each other's desires regarding family life.

21. **The need to be healthy**: Encourage a healthy lifestyle by engaging in physical activities together, preparing nutritious meals, and supporting each other's wellness.

22. **The need to be active**: Share active hobbies and interests, such as sports or outdoor adventures, to stay active and fit together.

23. **The need to be creative**: Explore your creativity together through artistic endeavours, crafts, or other creative outlets.

24. **The need to be reflective:** Create moments of introspection and self-discovery together. Engage in deep conversations about personal growth and self-awareness.

25. **The need to have romance**: Keep the romance alive by planning romantic dates, surprises, and gestures that show your affection and admiration for each other.

Remember that open communication is key to understanding and meeting each other's needs effectively. Regularly check in with your partner to ensure that you both feel valued and fulfilled in the relationship.

Activity: Identify you top 10 needs

Identify your and your partner's top 10 relationship needs. Discuss few strategies on how you can satisfy each other's needs:

Relationship Need	MINE	PARTNER
Need for Love		
Need for Value		
Need for Respect		
Need for Uniqueness		
Need for Appreciation		
Need for Admiration		
Need for Physical Intimacy		
Need for Care		
Need for Prioritization		
Need for Safety		
Need for Quality Time		

Need for Personal Space		
Need for Fun and Play		
Need for Social Connection		
Need for Career Fulfilment		
Need for Financial Security		
Need for Intellectual Stimulation		
Need for Communication		
Need for Family		
Need for Health		
Need for Activity		
Need for Creativity		
Need for Reflection		
Need for Romance		
Need for Honesty		

Trust

Trust is a fundamental component of any strong and lasting relationship. Trusting your partner in a relationship means having confidence, faith, and reliance on them in various aspects of the relationship.

Trusting your partner in a relationship means:

1. **Counting on Honesty**: It involves believing that your partner will consistently tell the truth and reveal important information. Honesty is not just about factual accuracy but also about being open and transparent about your inner world, including your thoughts, feelings, dreams, and desires.

2. **Expecting Faithfulness:** Trust includes the expectation that your partner will remain faithful to the commitment of the relationship. This means having confidence that your partner will not engage in romantic or sexual activities with others outside the relationship. It's about prioritizing the relationship and maintaining exclusivity.

3. **Earning Trust**: Trust is something that is earned over time through consistent actions and behaviours. It is not automatic but builds gradually as partners demonstrate their honesty, faithfulness, and reliability.

4. **Being Authentic**: In a trusting relationship, both partners should feel safe enough to be their true and authentic selves.

This involves revealing insecurities, weaknesses, and failures without fear of judgment or rejection. Trust encourages openness and vulnerability.

5. **Exercising Discretion:** While trust encourages openness, it also requires a degree of discretion. Partners should be mindful of each other's privacy and exercise discretion when it comes to sharing sensitive information or secrets. Respecting boundaries is essential for maintaining trust.

6. **Creating Emotional Safety**: Trust is closely linked to emotional safety. When you trust your partner, you feel emotionally secure and comfortable sharing your innermost thoughts and feelings. This emotional safety fosters a deeper connection and intimacy.

In summary, trusting your partner means having confidence in their honesty and faithfulness, which is earned through consistent actions and behaviours over time.

It's about creating an environment where both partners can be their authentic selves and feel emotionally safe, knowing that their vulnerabilities will be respected and valued. Trust is a fundamental component of a strong and lasting relationship.

Activity: Building trust on each other

Here are some questions that can help establish trust and understanding within a relationship:

- What does trust mean to you, and how important is it in a relationship?
- How do you feel about sharing financial details with your partner? What level of financial transparency is comfortable for you?
- Is there anything from your past relationships that you think is important to share with me?
- What are your thoughts on flirting with others while in a committed relationship?
- How much time spent apart from each other is acceptable to you?
- Do you believe it's necessary to share all your secrets with your partner? What kind of issues would you consider keeping private?
- How do you feel about your partner having close friends of the opposite sex? What level of intensity in these friendships is acceptable to you?
- Do you think there's a difference between a "white lie" and dishonesty? If so, where do you draw the line between them?

Personal boundaries

Personal space and boundaries are fundamental pillars in constructing robust and satisfying relationships. They serve as the bedrock for safeguarding individuality, upholding self-esteem, and cultivating a profound sense of security within a partnership. In a relationship where boundaries are respected, both individuals experience a profound sense of safety and confidence.

Here's why personal space and boundaries are important in relationships:

1. **Respect for Individuality:** Every person in a relationship has their unique interests, hobbies, and personal time. Respecting personal space allows individuals to pursue these activities, which are essential for personal growth and well-being. It acknowledges that both partners are separate individuals with their own needs and desires.

2. **Preservation of Self-Esteem**: Boundaries help protect self-esteem and self-worth. When boundaries are violated, it can lead to feelings of disrespect, inadequacy, or resentment. Respecting each other's boundaries is a way to affirm that both partners are valued and their feelings matter.

3. **Conflict Prevention**: Clear boundaries can help prevent misunderstandings and conflicts. When both partners understand each other's boundaries, they are less likely to inadvertently cross them, leading to fewer disagreements.

4. **Healthy Communication:** Establishing boundaries necessitates effective communication. Discussing personal space and boundaries encourages open and honest conversations. It enables partners to express their needs and expectations clearly, fostering understanding and compromise.

5. **Maintaining Attraction**: Paradoxically, maintaining individuality through personal space can enhance attraction within a relationship. When partners have time apart and then come together, it can rekindle the spark and create a sense of longing.

Activity: Understand each other's personal boundaries

Below, you'll find a set of questions designed to facilitate a meaningful dialogue with your partner regarding privacy and personal boundaries within your relationship. Engage in this discussion together, and brainstorm strategies to ensure mutual respect for each other's personal spaces.

1. How do you feel about sharing passwords or access to personal accounts, like email or social media, with your partner?

2. Do you think it's okay for partners to check each other's messages, emails, bank accounts or social media accounts without permission? If yes, when we have suspicion or have any concerns, how do you think we should tackle instead of checking each other's phones or emails?

3. Are there specific boundaries or privacy concerns you'd like to discuss or establish in our relationship?

4. What steps can we take to ensure that we respect each other's privacy while still maintaining trust and transparency?

5. How would you feel if I needed some personal space or alone time occasionally?

6. Are there any past experiences or situations that have influenced your perspective on personal boundaries?

7. How do you feel about spending time apart from each other, such as with friends or pursuing individual interests? What is your ideal balance between together time and personal time?

8. What actions or behaviours from your partner would make you feel that your personal boundaries are being respected?

9. What are some signs that you need personal space or time to yourself? How do you plan to communicate this to me?

10. Are there specific activities or hobbies that you consider as your personal time and space?

5 languages of love - expressing in your partners love language

Love languages, as elucidated by Dr. Gary Chapman, provide a profound understanding of the various ways individuals express and receive love within a relationship. Recognizing and appreciating these love languages can significantly enhance the depth and quality of your connection with your partner. Here are the five love languages:

1. **Words of Affirmation**: This love language revolves around verbal expressions of love and appreciation. People who resonate with this language value compliments, words of encouragement, and affectionate statements as significant tokens of affection.

2. **Acts of Service**: For individuals with this love language, actions speak louder than words. They feel most loved when their partner performs considerate acts of service, such as helping with chores, preparing breakfast, or lending a hand with various tasks.

3. **Receiving Gifts**: Some people perceive love most profoundly through the exchange of tangible gifts. It's worth noting that these gifts don't need to be extravagant; even small, thoughtful tokens convey meaningful affection.

4. **Quality Time**: Quality time enthusiasts yearn for undivided attention from their partner. To them, meaningful

conversations, shared experiences, and being fully present in each other's company hold utmost significance.

5. **Physical Touch**: Physical touch encompasses a spectrum of physical affection, ranging from hugs and kisses to holding hands and cuddling. For individuals with this love language, physical connection serves as a primary mode of expressing and receiving love.

Understanding your partner's primary love language enables you to convey your love in ways that deeply resonate with them, ensuring that they feel genuinely cherished. Equally important is conveying your own love language to your partner so that they can reciprocate in a manner that aligns with your preferences.

In relationships where the fundamental need is to feel loved and cared for, expressing love in a language that resonates with your partner functions like speaking their emotional dialect. It makes your affectionate gestures clearer, more impactful, and readily comprehensible.

For instance, if your partner's primary love language is "Acts of Service," they tend to express love through helpful actions. However, if your love language is "Words of Affirmation," you may not fully perceive or experience their love through these acts alone. You may long for verbal expressions of love and appreciation.

In this scenario, grasping your partner's love language bridges the gap. When you express love in their preferred language—offering compliments, words of encouragement, or verbal affirmations—it enables them to better understand

and internalize your affection. This not only guarantees that your love is received but also fosters a more profound emotional connection.

Similarly, when your partner comprehends your love language, they can reciprocate in a manner that deeply resonates with you. This shared understanding and effort to communicate in each other's love languages enhance the connection and generate feelings of being cherished, cared for, and adored.

Expressing love in your partner's love language doesn't entail altering your core self; it involves making deliberate gestures that demonstrate your love in ways meaningful to them.

It's a beautiful means of nurturing your emotional bond and cultivating a more loving, fulfilling relationship grounded in mutual understanding and appreciation. By conversing in each other's love languages, couples ensure their emotional cups of love remain replenished, nurturing a lasting and gratifying connection.

Activity: Find out each other's love language

Here are some questions that can help you and your partner identify each other's love languages:

1. Words of Affirmation:

   - Do you appreciate it when I give you compliments or praise?
   - How do you feel when I express my love and appreciation through words?
   - What kind of words or phrases make you feel most loved and valued?

2. Acts of Service:

   - Are there specific tasks or chores that I do which make you feel loved?
   - How does it make you feel when I take care of things for you?
   - What acts of service would you like me to do more often?

3. Receiving Gifts:

   - How do you feel when you receive a thoughtful gift from me?
   - Are there any gifts from the past that hold special meaning for you?
   - Do you appreciate surprises and tokens of affection?

4. Quality Time:

   - How important is spending quality time together to you?
   - What activities or experiences do you enjoy most when we're together?
   - How do you feel when we have meaningful conversations or share experiences?

5. Physical Touch:

   - What types of physical affection make you feel most loved and connected?
   - How important is physical intimacy in our relationship?
   - Are there specific ways you like to be touched or held?

These questions can serve as a starting point for discussing your love languages with your partner. Remember that understanding each other's love languages can greatly improve your relationship by ensuring your expressions of love are aligned with what truly resonates with your partner.

Chapter 3: Managing differences

Thus far, we've delved into various aspects of understanding each other, nurturing love, and building a strong foundation for a relationship. Now, let's turn our attention to potential factors that can give rise to differences, disagreements, and conflicts within a partnership if not approached positively.

It's important to note that differences in a relationship are not inherently negative. In fact, they can be incredibly healthy and enriching. These distinctions bring diversity, fresh perspectives, and opportunities for personal growth.

They challenge us to step outside our comfort zones and broaden our horizons. Varied viewpoints and experiences can lead to more comprehensive problem-solving and decision-making. Embracing differences means we have the chance to learn from one another and complement each other's strengths and weaknesses.

However, there is a critical caveat. While differences can be a source of growth and enrichment, they can also become problematic if they grow too substantial. When accommodating these differences requires compromising our authentic selves and core values, it's a cause for concern.

The key, therefore, is to strike a balance—a balance that allows us to celebrate our individuality and uniqueness while working together toward shared goals and values. It's about recognising that our differences can be a tremendous asset to our relationship, but also acknowledging when they start to impede our authenticity or challenge our fundamental values.

In the following sections, we will explore some common areas where differences and conflicts may arise in relationships and strategies for addressing them constructively. By understanding these potential pitfalls and learning how to navigate them effectively, we can strengthen the bonds of our partnership and ensure a healthier, happier future together.

Values

Values are fundamental beliefs and principles that guide our behaviour, choices, and expectations in life. They play a crucial role in shaping our vision of how we want to live and what we consider important.

While shared values can be a strong foundation for a harmonious relationship, differences in values can sometimes lead to conflicts. Let's explore each of the values you've mentioned and how they can potentially be sources of conflict:

1. **Social Values**: Social values encompass our beliefs and preferences regarding social interactions, friendships, and relationships with others. For example, one partner may highly value spending quality time with friends and maintaining an active social life, while the other may prioritise more alone time or one-on-one time with their partner. This difference in social values can lead to conflicts over how much time should be spent with friends and how much should be dedicated to the relationship.

2. **Monetary Values**: Monetary values revolve around how individuals view and handle money. Some people are savers, prioritizing financial security and long-term planning, while others are spenders, valuing immediate experiences and enjoyment. Conflict can arise when partners have differing financial priorities, spending habits, or financial goals, leading to disputes about budgeting, saving, or spending.

3. **Spiritual/Philosophical Values**: Spiritual and philosophical values encompass a person's beliefs about the meaning of life, existence, and their connection to a higher power or purpose. Conflicts may emerge if partners hold divergent spiritual or philosophical beliefs, especially if these beliefs are deeply rooted and non-negotiable.

4. **Ethical Values**: Ethical values pertain to principles of honesty, integrity, timeliness, loyalty, and a strong work ethic. When partners have differing ethical values, it can lead to conflicts over issues like honesty and trustworthiness.

For instance, one partner might value absolute honesty and transparency, while the other may believe in withholding certain information to protect feelings or maintain harmony.

5. **Family Values**: Family values relate to beliefs and expectations regarding family life, roles, and responsibilities. Conflict can arise when partners have varying views on family dynamics, such as the roles of spouses, expectations regarding parenting, or how much time should be spent with extended family members.

6. **Education Values**: Education values encompass attitudes toward learning, personal growth, and the pursuit of knowledge. Conflicts may occur if one partner places a high value on formal education and continuous learning, while the other may prioritise other life experiences or personal pursuits.

7. **Health and Fitness Values**: These values involve individual beliefs about maintaining physical and mental well-being. Conflicts can arise if one partner prioritises health and fitness, while the other may not place the same emphasis on exercise, nutrition, or self-care. These differences can lead to disagreements about lifestyle choices and habits.

For example, imagine a scenario where one partner highly values social connections and frequently wants to spend time with friends, while the other partner places a stronger emphasis on quality time together as a couple. This could result in conflicts over how weekends or evenings should be spent.

In another scenario, consider a situation where one partner is a dedicated saver, prioritising financial stability and long-term investments, while the other partner enjoys spending money on leisure and entertainment. These differing monetary values can lead to disagreements about budgeting, saving, and financial planning.

Ultimately, conflicts arising from differing values can be addressed through open and respectful communication. Partners should seek to understand each other's perspectives, find common ground, and be willing to compromise when necessary. By acknowledging these differences and finding ways to align their values and priorities, couples can navigate potential conflicts and strengthen their relationship.

Activity: Explore each other values

These questions can serve as conversation starters to delve deeper into each other's values. It's important to approach these discussions with empathy, openness, and a willingness to understand and respect each other's perspectives. Exploring these values together can help couples strengthen their connection and navigate potential conflicts more effectively.

1. Social Values:

- How do you prefer to spend your free time, especially when it comes to socializing with friends?
- What role do friendships and social connections play in your life?
- How would you like to balance spending time with friends and quality time together as a couple?

2. Monetary Values:

- What are your financial priorities and long-term goals?
- How do you approach budgeting, saving, and spending money?
- How would you like to handle financial decisions as a couple?

3. Spiritual/Philosophical Values:

- What are your spiritual or philosophical beliefs, and how important are they to you?

- How do you envision incorporating your beliefs into your life together?
- Are there any specific rituals or practices related to your beliefs that you'd like to share with your partner?

4. Ethical Values:

- What ethical principles do you consider essential in your life and relationships?

- How do you view honesty, transparency, and loyalty in a relationship?
   - Are there any ethical dilemmas or situations you'd like to discuss and align on as a couple?

5. Family Values:

   - What are your expectations and beliefs regarding family roles and responsibilities?
   - How would you like to navigate decisions related to parenting and extended family involvement?
   - Are there any specific family traditions or customs you'd like to incorporate into your relationship?

6. Education Values:

   - How do you view education and personal growth as part of your life journey?
   - Are there any educational or personal development goals you'd like to pursue together?
   - How can you support each other's learning and growth aspirations?

7. Health and Fitness Values:

   - What are your health and fitness priorities, and how do you maintain physical and mental well-being?
   - Are there any lifestyle choices or habits you'd like to share or adopt as a couple?

- How can you support each other in staying healthy and fit?

Common Interests

Common interests can be a powerful binding factor in any relationship, and they play a crucial role in creating a sense of connection and togetherness between partners. When two people share hobbies, passions, or activities they both enjoy, it provides them with a shared space to bond and create cherished memories.

These common interests can become a cornerstone of their relationship, strengthening their emotional connection and enhancing their overall sense of partnership.

However, what happens when partners' interests seem disconnected or vastly different from each other's? In such cases, taking proactive steps to form common interests becomes essential. Without this effort, differences in interests can potentially become a source of emotional disconnection or even lead to feelings of isolation within the relationship.

Shared interests can be a delightful and rewarding aspect of any relationship. They offer couples a shared space to bond, create memories, and enjoy each other's company. When partners have common interests, it provides an easy and enjoyable way to connect and spend quality time together.

Here are some categories of shared interests that couples often explore:

1. Recreation:

- Engaging in recreational activities like fishing, boating, hunting, or sports together can be a fantastic way to bond and enjoy the outdoors.
- Whether it's going on hikes, playing tennis, or attending sporting events, sharing recreational interests can create lasting memories and adventures.

2. Arts:

- Exploring the world of arts together, such as painting, sculpting, designing, or enjoying music and theatre, can be a source of inspiration and creativity.
- Couples can attend art exhibitions, visit museums, or even take up artistic hobbies as a way to connect through shared artistic expressions.

3. Hobbies:

- Shared hobbies like crafts, card games, or gardening can be a source of relaxation and fun.
- Working on DIY projects, playing board games, or tending to a garden together can offer a sense of accomplishment and shared enjoyment.

4. Lifestyle:

- Couples often bond over a shared lifestyle, such as a love for travel or a passion for dining and entertaining.
- Exploring new destinations, trying different cuisines, or hosting gatherings for friends and family can create cherished moments together.

Here's why forming common interests is important and how it can positively impact a relationship:

1. **Enhancing Emotional Connection**: Common interests provide couples with shared experiences that foster a deeper emotional connection. Engaging in activities both partners enjoy creates a sense of unity and reinforces their bond.

2. **Strengthening Couple Friendship**: Spending time together doing activities you both love can enhance your friendship as a couple. It allows you to connect on a friendlier level, enjoying each other's company and having fun together.

3. **Creating Shared Memories**: Common interests often lead to shared experiences and memories that you can cherish as a couple. These shared moments become part of your relationship's narrative and can strengthen your sense of togetherness.

4. **Improving Communication**: Engaging in activities you both enjoy provides opportunities for meaningful conversations. Whether you're discussing your shared

interests or simply chatting during these moments, it promotes open communication and understanding.

5. **Balancing Individuality and Togetherness:** While having common interests is valuable, it's also essential to maintain individuality within a relationship. Balancing shared activities with personal pursuits allows you both to grow as individuals while nurturing your connection as a couple.

6. **Spending Quality Time Together**: In our busy lives, finding time to spend together is crucial. Common interests offer a natural way to prioritize quality time as a couple, reinforcing your commitment to each other.

It's important to remember that forming common interests doesn't mean giving up your individual passions or hobbies. Instead, it involves exploring new activities or finding common ground within your existing interests. This effort requires a willingness to step out of your comfort zones, be open to each other's interests, and make compromises when needed.

Ultimately, the time and energy invested in forming common interests are an investment in your relationship's health and vitality. It's an acknowledgment of the value you place on your partnership and your commitment to nurturing it. By actively seeking shared activities and moments of joy, couples can create a deeper sense of togetherness and ensure that their relationship remains vibrant and fulfilling.

Activity: Discover common Interests

Here are some questions that can help couples explore and discover common interests. Find as many as possible.

1. What are some hobbies or activities you enjoy in your free time?
  - This question can reveal individual interests that you may have in common.

2. Have you ever tried something new or different that you found exciting or enjoyable?
  - Exploring new experiences together can lead to the discovery of shared interests.

3. Are there any childhood interests or hobbies you used to be passionate about?
  - Sometimes, revisiting childhood hobbies can spark shared interests.

4. Do you have any favourite movies, TV shows, or books that you could watch or read together?
  - Shared media interests can lead to enjoyable experiences as a couple.

5. What kind of outdoor activities do you find appealing?
  - Whether it's hiking, biking, or picnicking, outdoor activities can be a great way to bond.

6. Are there any sports or physical activities you'd like to try together?

- Sports and physical activities can provide a fun way to connect and stay active.

7. Do you both enjoy any particular types of music or concerts?
   - Attending concerts or listening to music you both love can be a shared passion.

8. Are there any local events or festivals you'd like to attend together?
   - Exploring your local community can lead to enjoyable shared experiences.

9. Have you considered taking up a class or workshop together to learn something new?
   - Learning a new skill or hobby as a couple can be an exciting adventure.

10. Are there any charitable or volunteer activities you're both interested in participating in?
   - Volunteering together can strengthen your bond while making a positive impact.

11. What are your travel interests, and do you have any dream destinations you'd like to visit together?
   - Traveling to new places can provide unforgettable shared experiences.

12. Are there any cuisines or cooking styles you both enjoy?
   - Cooking together or trying new cuisines can be a delicious way to connect.

13. Do you share any artistic interests, such as painting, crafting, or photography?
   - Exploring your creative sides together can lead to shared artistic endeavours.

14. Are there specific cultural or heritage-related activities you'd like to engage in together?
   - Celebrating your cultural backgrounds can be an enriching experience.

15. What are your thoughts on attending workshops or seminars related to personal growth or self-improvement as a couple?
   - Exploring personal growth together can strengthen your relationship.

These questions can serve as a starting point for couples to identify and develop common interests. Remember that the key is to be open to each other's preferences and be willing to try new things together. Over time, as you explore shared activities, you may discover new passions and hobbies that enrich your relationship.

Temperament and Personality traits

Differences in temperament and personality traits are common in any relationship and can contribute to its richness and depth. However, when these differences become extreme or are not managed effectively, they can lead to conflicts and dissatisfaction. Here, we explore some common personality traits and how they can impact couples:

1. Introverted/Extroverted:

- **Conflict Scenario**: An extroverted partner enjoys going out and socializing regularly, while their introverted partner prefers quiet evenings at home. This leads to misunderstandings and hurt feelings.

- **Resolution**: To address this conflict, the couple can work together to find a compromise that respects both partners' needs. They may decide to plan social activities on some weekends while dedicating other weekends to quiet, quality time at home.

Open communication is key, with each partner expressing their desires and boundaries. By finding a balance and understanding each other's preferences, they can create a harmonious dynamic that suits both introverted and extroverted tendencies.

2. Aggressive/Submissive:

  - **Conflict Scenario:** In this scenario, one partner tends to dominate conversations and decision-making, while the other feels unheard and undervalued.

  - **Resolution:** To address this issue, both partners can work towards a more balanced communication style. The dominant partner should practice active listening and allow space for the other to express themselves.

The submissive partner, on the other hand, can work on assertiveness by expressing their thoughts and needs clearly. Together, they can find compromise and ensure that both voices are heard and respected in the relationship.

3.Comical/Serious:

  - **Conflict Scenario:** One partner often uses humour as a coping mechanism during serious discussions or disagreements, while the other partner interprets this as dismissive, insensitive or hurt.

- **Resolution:** To address this issue, the couple can have an open conversation about how they both handle serious topics. They can acknowledge the importance of humour in diffusing tension but also set boundaries for when it's appropriate.

The partner using humour can work on actively listening to the serious concerns of their partner and respond with empathy. The serious partner can express their need for more sensitivity during certain discussions.

 Together, they can create a safe space where they can navigate both serious and light-hearted moments with mutual respect and understanding.

4. Analytical/Creative:

 - **Conflict Scenario:** In this scenario, one partner prefers a highly structured and organized approach to managing household finances, while the other partner is more spontaneous and creative in their financial decisions.

 - **Resolution:** To address this issue, the couple can have an open conversation about their financial goals and responsibilities. They can agree to create a financial plan that incorporates both structured budgeting and some flexibility for creative spending.

The analytical partner can manage the structured aspects of the budget, ensuring bills are paid on time and savings goals are met.

Meanwhile, the creative partner can have the freedom to allocate a portion of the budget for discretionary spending on creative pursuits or spontaneous experiences. This way, they can balance their financial responsibilities with the opportunity for creative expression and enjoyment.

5. Careful/Risk-Taker:

- **Conflict Scenario:** One partner tends to be financially prudent and is cautious about switching jobs or moving to a different city due to concerns about financial stability. The other partner is a risk-taker and believes that taking calculated risks is essential for career growth and personal fulfilment.

- **Resolution:** To navigate this conflict, the couple can consider a balanced approach. They might agree to conduct a thorough analysis of the potential job opportunities in the new city, including salary prospects, job market stability, and growth potential. Additionally, they can create a financial plan that accounts for possible risks, such as a job transition period or unexpected expenses.

This approach allows the risk-taking partner to pursue career opportunities while addressing the financial concerns of the more cautious partner. It emphasizes open communication and shared decision-making, ensuring that both partners' perspectives are considered in the process.

6. Easy-going/High Strung:

- **Conflict Scenario:** A high-strung partner becomes anxious and irritable during anything related with uncertainty, while the easy-going partner struggles to understand the intensity of their reaction.

- **Resolution: In** this scenario, the couple can address the conflict by acknowledging the differing stress responses. The high-strung partner can communicate their feelings and needs during stressful times, while the easy-going partner can offer emotional support and understanding.

They can discuss strategies for managing stress together, such as breaking tasks into manageable steps, practicing relaxation techniques, or seeking outside assistance if needed.

By openly addressing their reactions to stress and working together to navigate challenging situations like moving, they can strengthen their ability to support each other during stressful times, ultimately improving their relationship.

7. Conscientiousness Traits:

- Conflict Scenario: One partner is highly conscientious, valuing hard work, planning, and ambition, while the other partner is more easy-going and lacks discipline. This can result in frustration, as one partner may perceive the other as careless or lacking direction.

- Resolution: To resolve this conflict, the couple can acknowledge and appreciate each other's strengths and weaknesses. The conscientious partner can learn to be patient and understanding, recognizing that not everyone operates with the same level of structure and planning.

The easy-going partner can make an effort to be more organized and goal-oriented in specific areas where it matters. By finding common ground and supporting each other's growth, they can create a balanced and harmonious relationship that incorporates both conscientious and easy-going traits.

Activity: Find each other's personality and temperament

Here are some questions that can help you identify the personality and temperament of each other:

1. Introverted/Extroverted:

Social Interaction Preferences:

- In your ideal weekend, would you rather spend time with a small group of close friends or engage in a larger social event with acquaintances?

- How do you feel about attending gatherings where you might not know many people?

Personal Space and Solitude:

- What role does alone time play in your daily life, and how do you typically spend it?

- Can you describe a situation when you felt the need for personal space or solitude, and how did you handle it?

Socialising Styles:

- Do you tend to initiate conversations and interactions with others, or do you wait for others to approach you?

- How do you handle situations where you need to socialize but may feel drained or introverted at that moment?

2. Aggressive/Submissive:

Communication Style:

- How would you describe your communication style when expressing your thoughts and feelings?

- Are you more inclined to use assertive language and directness, or do you prefer a more gentle and indirect approach?

Decision-Making Preferences:

- When making decisions together, do you tend to take charge and lead the process, or do you prefer collaborative and consensus-based decision-making?

- How important is it for you to have your opinions and preferences considered in decision-making?

Conflict Resolution:

- Can you share an example of how you typically handle conflicts or disagreements in your relationships?

- Do you believe in finding compromises and common ground during conflicts, or do you prefer one person's viewpoint to prevail?

3. Comical/Serious:

Humour Preferences:

- Can you share a memorable moment when humour played a significant role in your life or a situation?

- Are there particular comedians, movies, or forms of humour that resonate with you the most?

Handling Serious Topics:

- How do you approach conversations about serious or sensitive subjects with your partner or in general?

- Can you describe a situation where maintaining a serious tone and focus was essential, and how did you handle it?

Balancing Humour and Seriousness:

- In your opinion, what's the right balance between humour and seriousness in a healthy relationship?

- Are there specific activities or hobbies that you enjoy together that incorporate humour or require a more serious approach?

4. Analytical/Creative:

Problem-Solving Styles:

- Can you share an example of a challenging problem or decision you've encountered and how you approached solving it?

- How do you handle situations where there's a need for both logical analysis and creative thinking?

Creative Outlets:

- Aside from your creative side, do you find enjoyment in structured or analytical activities as well?

- Can you describe a project or activity where you successfully combined your analytical and creative skills?

3. Balancing Structure and Spontaneity:

- In your ideal day or week, how do you balance structured, planned activities with spontaneous, creative pursuits?

- Are there areas of your life where you intentionally seek out opportunities for both analytical and creative expression?

5. Careful/Risk-Taker:

Risk-Taking Preferences:

- Can you recall a significant risk you've taken in your life, and what was the outcome?

- When it comes to trying new activities or experiences for **entertainment**, do you lean more toward adventure and novelty or familiarity and comfort?

Financial Decision-Making:

- How do you approach financial planning, especially in terms of saving, investing, or spending?

- Are there entertainment-related decisions where you're more inclined to be cautious, such as planning vacations or attending events?

Balancing Structure and Spontaneity:

- In your ideal day or week, how do you balance structured, planned activities with spontaneous, creative pursuits?

- Are there areas of your life where you intentionally seek out opportunities for both analytical and creative expression?

6. Easy going/High Strung:

Stress Response:

- Can you describe a recent situation that caused you stress, and how did you manage it?
- What are your primary sources of stress in daily life, and how do you cope with them?

Relaxation and Coping Strategies:

- Are there specific hobbies or activities you find especially relaxing and enjoyable?

- How do you unwind and recharge after a busy or stressful day?

Prioritising Calmness:

- In your ideal day, what elements contribute to a sense of calm and tranquillity?

- How does maintaining a peaceful environment at home or in your surroundings impact your overall well-being?

7. Conscientiousness Traits:

Work and Planning Preferences:

- How do you approach tasks and projects, and what role does planning play in your work style?

- Do you prefer to have a detailed plan before starting a task, or are you more comfortable with a flexible, spontaneous approach?

Goal Setting and Ambitions:

- What are some of your long-term goals, and how do you plan to achieve them?

- How do you define success, and how does it motivate your actions and decisions?

Time Management:

- How do you prioritize your daily tasks and responsibilities, and do you follow a strict schedule?

- Are you comfortable with making spontaneous changes to your plans, or do you prefer sticking to a predetermined routine?

Handling Responsibilities:

- How do you divide household or relationship responsibilities, and do you have specific expectations in this regard?
- How do you react when one partner is more focused on work and tasks, while the other values leisure and relaxation?

Dealing with Setbacks:

- How do you cope with setbacks or failures in your personal or professional life?

- Do you have strategies for maintaining motivation and resilience when facing challenges?

Growth and Adaptation:

- Are you open to trying new approaches or strategies when faced with obstacles, or do you tend to stick to what you know?

- How do you feel about stepping out of your comfort zone in pursuit of personal or professional growth?

These questions can serve as conversation starters to help you and your partner better understand each other's personality traits and temperaments. Keep in mind that individuals may exhibit a combination of these traits to varying degrees, and these traits can evolve over time.

Open and honest communication is key to navigating any differences and building a harmonious relationship.

Extended conversations

Having to choose one thing over another requires us to articulate our values and factors in our interests and temperament. Discuss the following hypothetical decisions. Create the conditions for each scenario that would allow you to make a decision of one over the other and then switch your position and state what conditions would be necessary to do so.

Accepting a Work Promotion vs. Living in a Less Desirable Geographic Location:

- What factors would make you prioritise accepting a work promotion over living in a less desirable location, and vice versa?

- How important is career advancement to you compared to living in a preferred geographic location?

- Can you identify circumstances under which you might change your decision?

Quitting a Job Due to Dissatisfaction vs. Staying for Financial Security:

- What aspects of job satisfaction matter most to you, and when would you consider quitting a job due to dissatisfaction?

- How does financial security rank in your priorities, and under what conditions would you prioritize it over job satisfaction?

- Are there specific financial or job-related factors that would influence your decision?

Taking a Walk or Run Together vs. Going on a Shopping Trip:

- How do you value physical activity and quality time together in comparison to shopping trips?

- Can you identify occasions when you might choose one activity over the other and the conditions that would lead to that decision?

Going on a Recreational Trip vs. Going to a Family Reunion:

- What importance do you place on spending time with family versus exploring new places and having recreational experiences?

- Are there specific family events or destinations that would sway your decision in one direction or the other?

Paying for Your Child's Education vs. Taking a Second Job:

- How do you prioritize investing in your child's education versus maintaining your current work-life balance?

- Can you pinpoint financial or educational circumstances that might influence your decision?

Having a Night Out with Friends vs. a Night with Just the Two of You:

- How do you weigh the benefits of socializing with friends against the importance of quality time as a couple?

- What factors or events might lead you to choose one option over the other on a particular occasion?

Purchasing a TV vs. Buying Season Tickets to a Sporting Event:

- How do you value entertainment options at home versus attending live sporting events?

- Are there specific sports or TV shows that hold particular significance for you, influencing your choice?

Visiting Old Friends vs. Visiting a Location You Have Never Been:

- How do you prioritize reconnecting with old friends compared to exploring new destinations?

- Can you identify situations that would lead you to choose one option over the other?

Allowing Your Child to Go to the Mall vs. Helping with Chores at Home:

- How do you balance giving your child independence and responsibility with maintaining household chores?

- Are there specific circumstances or tasks that would sway your decision in favour of one choice?

Taking a Family Vacation vs. a Vacation Just for the Two of You:

- How do you weigh the benefits of family bonding through vacations versus the importance of personal couple time?

- Can you pinpoint family events or occasions when one option might be preferred?

Attending a Family member's Retirement Party vs. Attending Your Child's Concert:

- How do you prioritise honouring social commitments versus supporting your child's activities?

- Are there specific considerations, like the significance of the event or prior commitments, that could affect your choice?

Adhering to a Budget vs. Impulse Spending:

- How do you view the importance of financial discipline compared to the occasional indulgence in impulse spending?

- Can you identify situations or financial goals that might sway your decision in one direction or the other?

Cuddling for the Night vs. Making Love:

- How do you value physical intimacy and emotional closeness in your relationship?

- Are there circumstances or emotional states that might lead you to prioritize one over the other on a given night?

Reading a Book vs. Doing a Project Around the House:

- How do you balance leisure activities like reading with productive projects and tasks at home?

- Can you identify specific situations or interests that would lead you to choose one activity over the other?

Having a Family Member Live with You vs. an Institutional Setting:

- How do you weigh the benefits of providing care and support within the family versus seeking institutional care for a family member?

- Are there considerations like the family member's needs or available support that might influence your decision?

Giving Money to a Charity vs. Giving Money to a Family Member:

- How do you prioritise charitable giving compared to providing financial support to family members?

- What specific charitable causes or family circumstances might sway your choice?

Spending the Holidays with One Side of the Family vs. the Other Side:

- How do you balance spending time with different sides of the family during the holidays?

- Are there specific family traditions or reasons that could influence your decision?

Likeability

Maintaining likability and courtesy within your home, especially with the person who means the most to you, is essential for a healthy and harmonious relationship. Here are some key aspects of being likable and practicing common courtesies within your home, along with explanations of how differences in these areas can lead to conflicts:

Good Grooming

Practicing good grooming habits, such as personal hygiene, cleanliness, and clothing choices, demonstrates respect for yourself and your partner.

Conflict may arise when one partner values meticulous grooming routines, specific clothing styles (e.g., traditional or western), and presentation when going out, while the other is more relaxed about it or has different clothing preferences.

These differences can lead to misunderstandings and potential discomfort, as well as extend to how each partner presents themselves when they leave the home.

Eating Styles

Differences in eating styles, such as some individuals making noises while chewing and others preferring quieter meals, can also lead to conflicts. Conflicting eating styles can cause discomfort during shared meals and may require open communication and compromises to find a middle ground that respects each partner's preferences.

Differences in Presentation at Home vs. When Going Out

It's common for individuals to have different presentation styles at home compared to when they go out. These differences may involve clothing choices, grooming routines, and behaviours.

Conflict may arise when one partner expects the other to maintain a consistently high level of presentation at home, similar to when going out, while the other partner is more relaxed about their appearance and behaviour in a home setting.

These differences can lead to misunderstandings and the need for communication and compromise to find a balance that suits both partners' comfort levels at home and in social settings.

Listening Carefully and Without Judgment

Actively listening to your partner, without interruption or judgment, fosters open communication and empathy. Conflict can emerge when one partner interrupts, criticizes, or passes judgment during conversations, hindering effective communication and causing frustration.

Using Good Manners

Practicing good manners in your interactions, including politeness, respect, and consideration for each other's clothing choices, accessories and behaviours when going out, creates a respectful and pleasant atmosphere. Conflicts may arise when one partner perceives the other's behaviour as rude or impolite, especially in social settings, leading to hurt feelings and tension

Balancing Cleanliness for Both

Agreeing on cleanliness standards for your shared living space is crucial for avoiding disagreements. Differences in cleanliness preferences, including how clothing items are stored or how clothing choices are managed in the home, can lead to ongoing conflicts about the state of the home environment.

Harmonising Volume

Being mindful of noise levels, especially during quiet times or when one partner needs concentration or rest, is considerate.

 Conflict may occur when one partner is significantly louder or fails to recognise the need for a quieter environment, causing disruptions and annoyance.

This consideration extends to behaviours when going out, ensuring that both partners are comfortable with the chosen activities and clothing choices for social settings.

Activity: Exploring likeabilities

Here are some questions that couples can use to identify their preferences and potential differences

1. Grooming:

- How important is a daily grooming routine to you?

- Are there specific grooming habits that you consider essential?

- How do you feel about maintaining personal hygiene standards?

- Do you have any preferences or habits related to clothing choices when going out or staying at home?

- Are there particular clothing styles that make you feel more comfortable or confident?

2. Eating Styles:

1. What are your eating preferences and habits, especially when dining at home?

- Are you vegetarian, non-vegetarian, or vegan?

- Do you have specific preferences for certain types of meals or cuisines?

2. Are there specific foods or cuisines that you enjoy or dislike?

- Are there any foods you particularly love and would like to have regularly?

- Are there foods or ingredients you dislike or are allergic to?

3. Do you have any dietary restrictions or preferences that we should consider when planning meals together?

- Are there certain days or periods when you prefer not to consume specific types of food, such as meat or dairy?

- Do you have any dietary restrictions due to health, religion, or personal choice?

4. How do you feel about making noise while eating, and do you prefer quieter meals?

- Are you comfortable with the sound of chewing and slurping during meals?

- Do you prefer quieter, more formal meals, or are you relaxed about mealtime noise?

5. What are your preferences when it comes to drinking alcohol or other beverages?

- Do you enjoy having alcoholic drinks occasionally, regularly, or not at all?

- Are there specific types of beverages you prefer or dislike?

6. Do you have any preferences or habits related to smoking or tobacco use?

- Are you a smoker or a non-smoker?

- How do you feel about smoking or tobacco use in your home or around you?

3. Differences in Presentation:

- Do you have differences in how you present yourself at home versus when going out in public?

- Are there specific reasons or occasions that influence your choice of presentation?

- How do you feel about your partner's presentation at home versus when going out?

- Can you identify scenarios where your preferences for presentation might vary?

Communication Styles:

- How would you describe your preferred communication style during discussions or disagreements?

- Do you feel that you listen actively and without judgment during conversations?

- Are there specific communication habits you would like to improve?

4. Manners:

Variations in Poise and Etiquette:

- Do you have a particular sense of poise or etiquette that you value in social situations?

- Are there specific social manners or etiquettes that you consider important when interacting with others?

- How do you feel about variations in poise and etiquette between you and your partner?

Fashion Sense and Style:

1. What role does fashion, including clothing, makeup, and accessories, play in your life, both at home and when going out?

2. Do you have specific fashion preferences, such as wearing makeup, jewellery, and accessories, or do you prefer simplicity and minimalism?

3. How do you react when your partner's fashion sense or style, including the choice to wear makeup or accessories, differs from your own?

Personal Style and Presentation:

1. How would you describe your personal style and presentation in various situations, including at home and in public?

2. Are there specific reasons or occasions that influence your choice of personal style and presentation, such as wearing makeup or jewellery?

3. How do you feel about your partner's personal style and presentation, especially if they differ from your own, including their choices regarding makeup, jewellery, and accessories?

Cleanliness

- How do you envision the level of cleanliness in our shared living space?

- Are there particular cleaning or tidying routines that you consider necessary?

- How do you react when the living environment doesn't meet your cleanliness standards?

Noise Levels

- Do you have specific preferences regarding noise levels in our home, especially during quiet times?

- How do you feel about maintaining a peaceful and quiet atmosphere in certain areas of the house?

- Are there activities or situations where you're comfortable with higher noise levels?

These questions can help couples open a dialogue about their preferences and expectations in various aspects of home life.

Lifestyle choices

Every relationship is a unique blend of two individuals, each with their own values, preferences, and approaches to life. These differences can enrich a partnership, but they can also lead to conflicts if not managed with care. In this exploration, we delve into various aspects of a relationship where differing viewpoints can spark disagreements and tensions.

From matters of faith and health to how couples care for each other during illness, these areas can challenge relationship harmony. Decisions about medication, cooking choices, and interactions with in-laws can be sources of conflict. Despite the potential challenges, these differences offer opportunities for growth, compromise, and stronger connections.

1. Consuming Pills vs. Natural Healing:

- Disagreements may occur regarding health and wellness approaches, with one partner favouring modern medicine and readily taking pills, while the other prefers natural or alternative healing methods.

- Conflicts might emerge when determining the appropriate course of action when dealing with health issues or ailments.

2. Caring When Sick vs. Allowing Independence

- Differences in providing care and emotional support when one partner is unwell can lead to conflicts.

- One partner may prefer nurturing and attending to the other's needs when sick, while the other may desire space and autonomy to recover independently.

3. Cooking Food at Home vs. Takeaways

- - Disagreements about food preferences and dietary choices can cause conflicts, especially when it comes to deciding whether to cook meals at home or order takeout.
- - Conflicts may stem from differences in culinary skills, health considerations, or budgetary concerns.

4. In-Laws Staying Together vs. Nuclear Family:

- - Deciding whether to live with or in close proximity to in-laws or maintain a nuclear family setup can be a significant source of conflict.
- - These conflicts often revolve around issues of privacy, autonomy, and differing cultural expectations.

5. Respecting Each Other: Avoiding Disregard in Family Settings

- Feeling unheard or devalued, especially in the presence of in-laws or extended family, can strain a relationship.

- Conflicts may arise when partners unintentionally or intentionally disregard each other's perspectives or needs, leading to feelings of disrespect and hurt.

Addressing these potential areas of conflict requires open and empathetic communication. Couples can work towards finding compromises and solutions that respect each other's values, preferences, and boundaries while nurturing a healthy and harmonious relationship.

Activity: Explore your preferences

These questions can serve as conversation starters for couples to explore their differences, preferences, and expectations in these potential areas of conflict. Open and honest discussions can help couples find common ground and develop strategies for addressing these differences positively.

Healthcare and Medication:

- What are your views on healthcare and using medication for various health issues?
- Do you believe in natural healing and letting the body recover on its own, or do you prefer medical intervention?
- How would you like us to approach healthcare decisions for ourselves and our family?

Caring During Sickness:

- How do you typically provide support and care when your partner is unwell?
- Are there specific ways you prefer to be cared for when you're not feeling well?
- What are your expectations regarding emotional support during sickness?

Food and Dining Preferences:

- How important is home-cooked food to you, and what role does it play in your life?
- Do you have specific dietary preferences or restrictions that should be considered in our meals?
- How do you feel about occasional takeout or dining out?

Living Arrangements:

- What are your thoughts on living arrangements, such as having in-laws live with us versus having a nuclear family setup?
- Are there specific boundaries or considerations you'd like to discuss regarding our living situation?
- How can we ensure that our living arrangements are comfortable and harmonious for both of us?

Public vs. Private Support:

- How do you feel about receiving emotional support in public versus in private?
- How can we ensure that we both feel respected and valued in various social settings?
- Are there situations where you'd prefer not to be corrected or criticised in front of others, especially family or friends?

Chapter 4: Joint decision making

The topics covered so far provide a foundation for couples or to be couples to deeply understand each other. Now, let's explore discussions that can serve as a guide for couples to unite as a cohesive unit and navigate any potential differences together.

Marriage or living together with your partner, introduces a new dimension to decision-making, with a multitude of daily choices that reflect your values, needs, and moods. In this context, many of the issues discussed earlier can become prominent factors in the decision-making process.

The ideal scenario involves both partners feeling at ease expressing their needs in a non-confrontational manner. Effective decision-making as a couple hinges on compromise, kindness, thoughtfulness, strong communication skills, heartfelt conversations, and courteous negotiations.

These elements collectively contribute to a harmonious and cooperative approach to navigating life's decisions together.

Children

Among life's most profound and enduring decisions, the choice to have children stands unique. It's a decision that carries permanence and irreversibility. Unlike changing jobs, careers, locations, or even life partners, bringing a child into the world means embracing a lifelong role as a parent. Barring unforeseeable tragedies, parenthood means being there, unwaveringly, for your child—providing love, guidance, and care.

At its core, parenting is about ensuring your child knows they are loved unconditionally, even in moments of mistakes and missteps. It's about making their well-being a top priority and nurturing their journey towards independence—a delicate and continuous process. Building trust serves as the bedrock of parenting, fostering a child's physical, intellectual, social, and emotional development.

The path of parenthood demands boundless patience, self-sacrifice, and a substantial investment of time. It has the power to either deepen the bond between partners or place strains upon it, contingent on the health and functionality of the relationship. Parental responsibilities bring into sharp focus the values and priorities of both individuals, underscoring the importance of alignment on crucial aspects of child-rearing.

In today's ever-evolving world, modern scenarios have arisen, further complicating the decision-making surrounding parenthood. Couples now grapple with choices concerning the method of childbirth, contemplating options like natural birth, surrogacy, or other artificial means. Additionally, decisions revolve around feeding choices, weighing the options between breastfeeding and relying on external sources of nutrition.

Modern parenting also ushers in a range of dilemmas. These include shared parenting responsibilities, potential reliance on external assistance or childcare, and the involvement of extended family, including grandparents, in raising the child. Couples may need to address issues like career adjustments, co-parenting arrangements, and even unconventional parenting roles, such as "penguin dads" who take on a more active role in childcare.

These diverse scenarios encompass a spectrum of complexities, necessitating thorough consideration and open communication between partners. Choices made in the realm of parenthood wield a profound and enduring impact on a couple's life journey.

Therefore, thoughtful decision-making, compromise, and a shared understanding of values and priorities stand as indispensable components for successfully navigating the intricate path of parenthood together.

Activity: Discussion about children

Below questions can provide a valuable foundation for discussions between partners considering parenthood:

1. Desire for Children and Number

- Why do you want to have children, and what are your motivations?

- How many children do you envision having, and why?

2. Expectations of Parenthood

- What do you imagine it will be like to be a parent?

- What are your hopes and fears about parenthood?

3. Expectations of Your Partner

- What do you expect from your partner as a parent, both in terms of responsibilities and emotional support?

- How can your partner best support you during this journey?

4. Accommodations for Children

- What changes or accommodations are you willing to make in your home to ensure a safe and nurturing environment for your children?

- How do you foresee adjustments in your financial, career, and lifestyle choices to accommodate children?

5. Parenting Style and Values

- What type of disciplinarian do you think you'll be, and what are your disciplinary philosophies? (Authoritative Discipline: Balanced; Permissive Discipline: Indulgent; Authoritarian Discipline: Strict)

- What core values and principles do you want to instil in your children, and how do you plan to model them?

6. A Typical Day with Children

- Describe what you expect a typical day with your children to be like.

- How do you envision daily routines and activities?

7. Family Traditions and New Creations

- What family traditions from your own upbringing do you want to carry on with your children?

- Are there any new traditions or experiences you wish to create as a family?

8. Admiration for Parenting

- Share with each other who you admire as a parent and why.

- What qualities or actions of these admired parents resonate with you?

Discussing these questions can help partners gain a deeper understanding of each other's perspectives and expectations regarding parenthood. It also provides an opportunity to align on key aspects of parenting and plan for the exciting journey ahead.

Finances

Within any relationship, financial matters hold a significant role, capable of both fortifying the bond between partners and introducing divisions. Money symbolises not only financial security but also personal success and identity, making it a sensitive yet important topic to consider.

Imagine this scenario: a couple originates from distinct financial backgrounds and bears dissimilar financial values. While one partner prioritizes saving for the future, the Money symbolizes other leans towards indulging in immediate pleasures.

These divergent money mindsets can lead to conflicts when it comes to allocating their financial resources—whether for daily expenses, savings, investments, or discretionary spending.

For instance, one partner may be committed to building a financial safety net by setting aside a portion of their income each month, while the other views money as a means to savour the present and prefers spontaneous purchases and experiences.

This contrast in perspectives can create challenges in striking a balance between immediate enjoyment and long-term financial security. Shared financial goals and responsibilities within a relationship can also be a source of stress.

Discussions concerning joint expenses like rent, utilities, and daily living costs can become tedious if not approached thoughtfully. Similarly, managing shared debts, such as student loans or credit card balances, can lead to conflicts if both partners do not see eye to eye on financial strategies.

Now, contemplate the intersection of individual financial goals and aspirations. While one partner dreams of homeownership or embarking on a global adventure, the other's ambitions may incline towards further education or early retirement. These varying visions can complicate financial planning, necessitating meticulous communication and compromise.

In essence, money constitutes a multifaceted element within any relationship, reflecting personal values, aspirations, and lifestyle choices. To navigate this terrain successfully, open and honest discussions concerning financial goals, spending habits, and budgeting are crucial.

It is essential to collaborate in creating a financial plan that respects each other's values while ensuring financial stability and mutual growth within the relationship. By doing so, couples can fortify their financial foundation and enhance their partnership. However, finances in a relationship extend beyond individual spending—they also encompass shared responsibilities. When partners merge their lives, they typically combine their financial resources and make decisions collectively.

Shared responsibilities encompass various aspects

1. **Joint Expenses:** Partners frequently share the financial load of essential living expenses, such as rent or mortgage payments, utilities, groceries, and transportation. Deciding how to distribute these costs or contribute to a shared account is a pivotal aspect of financial planning.

2. **Debt Management:** Couples may grapple with shared debts, such as student loans, car loans, or credit card balances. Deciding how to handle and pay off these debts, as well as whether to take on new ones, requires open communication and alignment in financial goals.

3. **Savings and Investments:** Preparing for the future often involves shared savings and investment goals. This could encompass building an emergency fund, saving for a home, or investing in retirement accounts. Agreeing on how to allocate resources for these goals is crucial for long-term financial stability.

4. **Financial Goals**: Couples should discuss their individual and shared financial aspirations, ranging from short-term

objectives like a vacation to long-term plans like homeownership, children's education, or retirement. Aligning these goals and crafting a financial roadmap is essential.

Beyond these shared financial goals, couples also face responsibilities that extend to caring for their parents and other family members. These responsibilities encompass:

1. **Elderly Parents**: If one or both partners have aging parents, discussions about providing financial support or caregiving responsibilities may arise. This can impact the couple's budget and long-term planning.

2. **Children's Education:** Planning for a child's education, whether through savings, investments, or financial aid, is a significant financial responsibility that couples must address.

3. **Healthcare Costs:** Coping with unexpected medical expenses for family members can strain a budget. Couples should contemplate how to handle such situations, including health insurance coverage and savings for medical emergencies.

4. **Charitable Giving:** Couples may share a commitment to charitable causes. Deciding how to allocate resources for philanthropic efforts can be an important part of financial planning.

Supporting a Stay-at-Home Partner for Financial Empowerment:

When considering the possibility of one partner becoming a stay-at-home partner, whether due to starting a family, other life changes, or even as a choice at the beginning of marriage, discussions should extend beyond financial dependency to ensuring financial empowerment.

It's a shared responsibility to make the stay-at-home partner feel empowered, valued, and capable of managing both financial and non-financial aspects of life together. Here are some critical considerations:

1. **Joint Decision-Making**: The decision for one partner to stay at home should be made jointly, with open and honest communication. Both partners should express their desires, concerns, and expectations regarding this choice. This ensures that the decision aligns with both partners' values and goals.

2. **Financial Transparency**: Maintaining financial transparency is crucial. Both partners should have a comprehensive understanding of the family's financial situation, including income, expenses, savings, investments, and any outstanding debts. Regular discussions about finances help in making informed decisions.

3. **Budgeting Together**: Establishing a clear and mutually agreed-upon budget is essential. This budget should outline how household expenses, savings, and discretionary spending will be managed. Regularly reviewing and adjusting the budget together ensures that it reflects evolving needs and goals.

4. **Financial Contributions**: Even if one partner is the primary breadwinner while the other chooses to stay at home, it's essential to discuss how the stay-at-home partner can continue to make financial contributions:

  - Shared Responsibilities: The stay-at-home partner can actively participate in managing household finances, including bill payments, tracking expenses, and finding ways to economize.

  - Personal Projects: Encouraging the pursuit of personal projects or hobbies that have the potential to generate income. This not only contributes to the family's financial well-being but also allows the stay-at-home partner to explore their passions.

5. **Maintaining Financial Independence**: Financial empowerment means that the stay-at-home partner retains a sense of financial independence. This can be achieved by:

  - Individual Savings: Encouraging the stay-at-home partner to maintain personal savings accounts. This enables them to save for personal goals, emergencies, or investments.

- Investing in Growth: Supporting opportunities for the stay-at-home partner to invest in their personal growth, such as pursuing further education, skill development, or entrepreneurial ventures.

6. **Family Responsibilities**: Acknowledging that family responsibilities extend beyond financial matters. If the stay-at-home partner is responsible for taking care of the home, children, or elderly.

Activity: Discuss your financial planning and lifestyle

In the journey of building our life together, it's essential to have open and meaningful discussions about our desired lifestyle and how we plan to achieve it financially.

These discussions will serve as the foundation for our financial well-being and overall happiness as a couple.

1. **Desired Lifestyle:** Let's start by talking about our desired lifestyle. What kind of life do we envision for ourselves as a couple and for our family, if we plan to have one? Discussing

the lifestyle we aspire to will help us set clear financial goals and priorities.

2. **Savings Plan**: Creating a savings plan is crucial for our financial security and achieving our goals. How do we plan to save for short-term needs and long-term aspirations like homeownership, travel, or retirement? Let's outline a savings strategy that aligns with our objectives.

3. **Budgeting**: Establishing a budget is an effective way to manage our finances. Do we intend to have a budget, and if so, how will we determine it? Discussing our budgeting approach will help us track our expenses and ensure that we're meeting our financial goals.

4. **Managing Finances**: Will one of us take more control over financial matters, or do we prefer to make financial decisions jointly? Additionally, should we have individual or joint checking accounts? Clarifying these aspects will help us establish a financial management system that works for both of us.

5. **Spending Priorities**: What are our spending priorities as a couple? Identifying where we want to allocate our financial resources, whether it's for travel, education, or other goals, will guide our spending decisions.

6. **Income Disparities**: It's possible that one of us may earn more than the other. How will this income disparity affect our financial decisions? Discussing this openly will help us

ensure that both partners feel valued and included in financial matters.

7. **Creating Value**: Besides earning income, each of us brings unique skills, interests, and contributions to our partnership. How can we leverage these strengths to create additional value in our lives, whether through shared hobbies, side projects, or other means?

8. **Charitable Giving**: Giving back to the community and supporting charitable causes can be an important part of our financial plan. How much do we intend to allocate for charitable donations, and which causes do we want to support?

By engaging in these discussions and aligning our financial goals, we can build a strong financial foundation for our life together. It's crucial that we continue to communicate openly about money matters, make joint decisions, and work as a team to achieve the life we envision.

Career Planning and Life Choices

As couples embark on their journey together, it's essential that they engage in open and thoughtful conversations about their career aspirations and the life choices that will shape their path as a couple. These discussions will help couples align their goals and decisions, ensuring a harmonious and fulfilling shared future.

1. **Career Aspirations**: Let's kickstart the conversation by sharing their individual career aspirations and long-term goals. What do each of them envision professionally, both in the short term and down the road? Understanding each other's career plans will strengthen their support for one another.

2. **Embracing Entrepreneurship**: Entrepreneurship is a significant career choice that merits careful consideration. Are there entrepreneurial ventures they're interested in, either jointly or independently? Couples should discuss how to navigate the challenges and benefits of entrepreneurship while maintaining financial stability.

3. **Career Breaks**: There may come a time when one partner desires a career break, whether for personal growth, further education, or other reasons. How do they feel about this possibility? It's crucial for couples to explore their willingness to support each other during career breaks and how they'll manage finances during these periods.

4. **Decision-Making Approach**: When it comes to career planning and life choices, what decision-making approach shall they adopt? Should they make decisions collaboratively, with both partners actively participating in discussions and choices? Clarifying their decision-making process will ensure mutual respect and understanding.

5. **Mutual Support**: Expressing how they can best support each other in their respective career journeys is paramount. What emotional and practical support can couples offer as each partner pursues their professional goals?

6. **Work-Life Balance**: Striking a balance between their careers and personal lives is essential for their well-being as a couple. How can couples effectively manage their time and responsibilities to nurture a satisfying personal life alongside their professional endeavours?

7. **Financial Preparedness**: Career decisions often carry financial implications. How shall couples navigate financial considerations during career transitions, whether it involves starting a new business, returning to school, or adapting to a single income in a stay-at-home context?

Engaging in these conversations and seeking common ground will enable couples to chart a course for their careers and life choices that respects their individual aspirations while honouring their shared journey. Through transparent communication, empathy, and a shared commitment to collaboration, couples can make informed decisions that lead to a fulfilling life together.

Activity: Discussion on career choices

Here are some questions that partners can ask to engage in discussions about career planning and life choices:

1. **Career Aspirations:**

   - What are your short-term and long-term career goals?

   - How do you envision your professional growth in the coming years?

   - Are there specific industries or roles you aspire to work in?

2. **Entrepreneurship:**

   - Have you considered any entrepreneurial ventures or business ideas?

   - How do you feel about the risks and rewards of entrepreneurship?

   - Are there joint business opportunities we'd like to explore?

3. Career Breaks:

- Have you ever thought about taking a career break for personal growth, further education, or other reasons?

- How would you manage finances during a career break?

- What kind of support would you need from your partner during this time?

4. Stay-at-Home Partner:

- How do you feel about the possibility of one partner staying at home, especially if we decide to start a family?

- What are your expectations and concerns regarding this arrangement?

- How should roles and responsibilities be divided in this scenario?

5. Decision-Making Process:

- What approach should we take when making decisions about our careers and life choices?

- Should decisions be made jointly, or do you prefer a more individual decision-making process?

- How can we ensure that both partners feel involved and valued in the decision-making process?

6. Supporting Each Other:

- How can we best support each other in pursuing our career goals?

- What forms of emotional and practical support do you need from your partner?

- Are there specific challenges you anticipate, and how can we address them together?

7. Work-Life Balance:

- What strategies do you think would help us achieve a balance between work and personal life?

- How can we manage our time and responsibilities to ensure a fulfilling personal life alongside our careers?

8. Financial Considerations:

- How would we handle finances during significant career transitions, such as starting a new business or going back to school?

- Are there financial safety nets or plans we should put in place for such situations?

- What is our strategy for managing finances if one partner becomes a stay-at-home partner?

These questions can serve as a starting point for meaningful discussions about career planning and life choices. It's important for partners to listen actively, express their thoughts and concerns openly, and work together to find solutions that align with their individual aspirations and their shared journey as a couple.

Spiritual, religious and philosophical Beliefs

A religious or spiritual life can be so incredibly important to some and not to others, but we all have some form of a philosophy we adhere to and it can dramatically shape your life choices.

Activity: share your preferences

Expectations of Support:

Begin by discussing your expectations regarding support for your religious or spiritual beliefs. It's crucial to understand each other's needs and boundaries in this regard. Do you expect active participation in each other's faith, or are you more comfortable with a respectful coexistence of your beliefs? These conversations will lay the foundation for a harmonious integration of your spirituality into your relationship.

Significant Rituals and Practices:

Delve into the specific religious rituals or practices that hold significance for each of you. Understanding what these mean to you individually can help you appreciate and respect the traditions and customs that are integral to your lives.

Incorporating Beliefs into Your Relationship:

To ensure a seamless integration of your religious or spiritual beliefs into your relationship and future family life, brainstorm strategies. For example, decide on how you want to celebrate religious holidays or observe personal spiritual practices.

These discussions can help you create a supportive and inclusive environment where your beliefs can coexist harmoniously.

Addressing Differences and Family Expectations:

Recognise that there may be differences in your spiritual or religious beliefs, rituals, and family expectations. Discuss how you can support and respect each other's decisions in areas where your beliefs diverge.

Explore ways to find common ground, build understanding, and navigate potential challenges that may arise from varying backgrounds or family traditions.

Rituals and Practices:

If you follow specific religious or spiritual rituals, share these practices and their significance. Discuss how you would like to incorporate these rituals into your shared life or respect each other's practices if they differ.

Balancing Roles and Responsibilities in Household

As partners in this journey of life together, It's important to recognise that certain tasks and responsibilities are essential for the seamless functioning of a household.

To ensure that these responsibilities are handled effectively and do not become sources of stress in a relationship, it is imperative for couples to engage in open and constructive discussions.

Through these discussions, couples can establish a harmonious division of labour that takes into account individual preferences, strengths, and schedules.

By engaging in discussions with respect, empathy, and a shared commitment to partnership, couples can establish a balanced and supportive approach to sharing the responsibilities of life together.

This collaborative effort ensures that neither of the partners feels overwhelmed and that both of you thrive in an atmosphere of shared contribution and understanding.

Activity: Understanding Each Other's Preferences

Here are some key areas that significantly impact daily lives. Delve into each of these and explore how couples can equally share the responsibilities:

Parenting: Parenthood is a shared journey that necessitates the active involvement of both partners. While the specific tasks related to parenting may vary, encompassing childcare, school involvement, or engagement in extracurricular activities, it is paramount that both the partners actively participate in decision-making and daily caregiving.

Generating Income: The process of generating income is a crucial aspect of lives. Discuss whether one person's career takes precedence over the other and how both can find a balance that respects each other's career goals and aspirations.

House Chores: House maintenance and chores are essential for the upkeep of home's appearance and functionality. Discuss individual preferences and schedules to determine how couples can divide or share these responsibilities in a fair and practical manner.

Food Preparation: Planning and preparing meals are tasks that can be shared based on culinary skills and preferences.

Brainstorm and establish a system where couples can take turns or collaborate in the kitchen, ensuring that mealtime is both enjoyable and manageable.

Cleaning: Maintaining clean and organised living spaces benefits everyone in household. It's crucial to discuss and explore how couples can divide cleaning tasks fairly, taking into consideration each partner's strengths and availability.

Financial Matters: Managing finances, which includes paying bills and creating a budget, plays a pivotal role in having financial stability. Have conversations about how couples can collaboratively handle these responsibilities, fostering transparency and aligning with combined and individual financial goals.

Laundry: Laundry is a routine task that can be shared based on availability and preference. Discuss and devise a system that works for both couples, whether it involves taking turns or dividing specific aspects of laundry care.

Home Maintenance: Home maintenance tasks, such as repairs and upkeep, are essential for our living environment's functionality and safety. Discuss how both of you intend to address these tasks, whether through DIY efforts, hiring professionals, or a combination of both, to ensure home remains a comfortable and secure haven.

Navigating Joint Responsibilities: Building Closer Connections in Your Partnership

In a relationship, how responsibilities are shared can profoundly influence the overall harmony. When one partner enjoys relaxation time while the other is burdened with the majority of family duties or left to navigate the complexities of child-rearing solo, whether they are stay-at-home or working it can lead to friction in relationships.

Or when one partner takes majority of burden of tending to the needs of the family while the other travels extensively, it can strain the bonds of connection and breed dissatisfaction. To address these challenges and strengthen your connection, consider the following strategies:

1. **Open Communication**: Establish open and honest communication to discuss and understand each other's needs, preferences, and challenges. Create a safe space for expressing feelings and concerns without judgment.

2. **Shared Responsibilities:** Ensure that responsibilities are shared fairly. If one partner enjoys relaxation time, find ways to balance this by sharing household chores or childcare duties. Recognize and appreciate the importance of each other's downtime.

3. Quality Time Together: Prioritise quality time together. Amidst busy schedules, carve out moments for shared activities, conversations, or simply being present with each other. These moments of connection strengthen the emotional bond and serve as a reminder of the importance of the relationship.

4. Scheduled Breaks: For the partner taking on more responsibilities, schedule breaks or relaxation time. This ensures that both partners have moments of rejuvenation and helps prevent feelings of burnout.

5. Regular Check-ins: Schedule regular check-ins to assess the distribution of responsibilities. This provides an opportunity to make adjustments as needed, ensuring that the workload remains balanced and manageable for both partners.

6. Supportive Partnerships: Be supportive of each other's endeavours. Recognise and celebrate each other's achievements, both in personal pursuits and shared responsibilities. A supportive attitude fosters a sense of teamwork and mutual appreciation.

7. Build a Support System: Establish a support system, whether it involves seeking assistance from extended family, friends, or considering professional help for specific tasks. Having additional support can lighten the load and create a more balanced environment.

8. Understanding Roles: When one partner stays at home, ensure that the other understands the challenges and efforts involved. Recognise and appreciate the contributions of the partner managing home responsibilities.

9. Flexibility and Adaptability: Life circumstances change, and so can the demands on your time and energy. Periodically reassess your responsibilities and be open to adjusting taking over responsibilities and the distribution based on evolving needs, work commitments, or changes in family dynamics.

10. Define Boundaries: Establish clear boundaries regarding work commitments and personal time. While pursuing hobbies and career aspirations is essential, setting limits ensures that the relationship remains a priority. Balance is key, and both partners should be considerate of each other's need for personal space.

11. Supportive Environment: Foster a supportive environment where both partners feel valued and acknowledged for their contributions. This includes recognising the challenges faced by the partner who may be shouldering the majority of responsibilities, whether they are a stay-at-home or managing work commitments.

By incorporating these strategies, couples can navigate the complexities of shared responsibilities, where partner feels seen, heard, and appreciated.

Balancing Roles and Responsibilities in Pet Care

Just as in other aspects of life together, couples must also consider the tasks and responsibilities related to their beloved pets. To ensure that pets receive the love and care they deserve without becoming a source of tension, it's essential for couples to openly discuss and establish a balanced approach to pet care.

Activity: Understanding Each Other's Preferences

Here are some key areas related to pet care that couples should discuss and find equitable solutions for:

1. Do both partners have a preference for owning pets? If so, what types of pets do you both like, and why?

2. When it comes to dogs, do you have specific preferences regarding their size (small, medium, or large) or breed? What factors influence these preferences?

3. If you're considering cats as pets, do you have any specific

preferences regarding their age (kittens vs. adult cats) or breed?

4. Are there any other animals or pets that one or both of you are particularly fond of, such as birds, rabbits, reptiles, or exotic pets?

5. Have you had previous experiences with pets, and if so, how have these experiences shaped your preferences and expectations for pet ownership?

6. What are the primary reasons for wanting to bring a pet into your lives? Is it for companionship, security, emotional support, or any other specific reasons?

7. Are there any concerns or reservations about pet ownership that you'd like to discuss? For example, considerations related to allergies, lifestyle, or living arrangements.

8. How do you envision integrating pets into your daily routines and lifestyles? What roles and responsibilities do you foresee in caring for your pets?

9. Are there any specific pet-related activities or experiences you look forward to sharing as a couple, such as outdoor adventures, training, or simply spending quality time together with your pets?

10. If there are differences in your pet preferences, how do you plan to find common ground and make decisions regarding the type of pet(s) to bring into your home?

Discussing these questions will not only help couples understand each other's pet preferences but also lay a solid foundation for responsible and enjoyable pet ownership that aligns with their shared goals and values.

Navigating Sexual Compatibility, Consent, and Romantic Intimacy

Fostering an environment of comfort, consent, and romantic intimacy is vital for a fulfilling and healthy sexual relationship. Here are some important considerations and tips for couples:

1. **Go at Your Own Pace:** Every individual has their own comfort level and desires when it comes to intimacy. It's crucial to go at a pace that both partners are comfortable with. Never pressure or rush each other into any sexual activity. Prioritize mutual consent and respect for each other's boundaries.

2. **Open Communication**: Initiating conversations about sex can be challenging but is essential for understanding each other's desires and boundaries. Create a safe space where

both partners can openly discuss their preferences, fantasies, and concerns without judgment.

3. **Romantic Gestures:** Incorporating romance into your relationship can enhance intimacy. Surprise each other with thoughtful gestures like love notes, romantic dinners, or planning a special date night. These actions can help maintain emotional connection and anticipation.

4. **Importance of Foreplay**: Foreplay plays a crucial role in building anticipation and increasing pleasure. Spend time on sensual activities that create excitement and enhance the overall experience. Listen to each other's cues and adjust your actions accordingly.

5. **Respect and Consent**: Always prioritize consent. Each partner should feel comfortable saying "no" at any point if they are not ready or willing to engage in sexual activity. Respecting each other's boundaries and choices is fundamental to a healthy sexual relationship.

6. **Creating a Romantic Atmosphere:** Pay attention to the ambiance in your bedroom. Lighting, scents, and music can set the mood for a romantic evening. Experiment with creating a cosy and intimate atmosphere that appeals to both partners.

7. **Medical Considerations**: If either partner is experiencing sexual health challenges, such as erectile dysfunction, discuss the issue openly and consult a healthcare

professional. Medications like Viagra can be helpful in such cases but should be used under medical guidance.

8. **Explore Together:** Sexual compatibility often involves exploration and trying new things together. Be open to experimenting with different techniques, positions, or fantasies that both partners are comfortable with.

9. **Emotional Connection**: Maintain a strong emotional connection outside the bedroom. Quality time, affection, and emotional intimacy contribute to a more satisfying sexual relationship.

Remember that a healthy sexual relationship is built on trust, respect, communication, and mutual consent.

By creating a romantic atmosphere, engaging in open and honest conversations, prioritizing foreplay, and respecting each other's choices and boundaries, couples can enhance their sexual compatibility and intimacy while maintaining a loving and fulfilling relationship.

Activity: Exploring and understanding each other's desires

Here are some questions for couples to explore and enhance their understanding of each other's desires and boundaries in a healthy sexual relationship:

1. What does intimacy mean to you? Understanding each other's definitions of intimacy can help align your expectations.

2. How do you prefer to initiate sexual activity or show desire? Discuss your preferred ways of expressing desire to ensure both partners feel desired and appreciated.

3. What are your boundaries and limits when it comes to intimacy? Openly share your boundaries and respect each other's limits to prioritize consent.

4. Are there specific fantasies or desires you'd like to explore together? Sharing fantasies can lead to exciting and fulfilling experiences if both partners are comfortable.

5. What turns you on or enhances your pleasure during sexual activity? Discuss specific techniques, touches, or actions that bring pleasure.

6. How do you communicate your desires and needs during intimacy? Effective communication is key to ensuring both partners are satisfied.

7. What are your thoughts on introducing romance into our sexual relationship? Explore ways to add romance, such as surprise gestures or special date nights.

8. Do you have any concerns or challenges related to sexual health or performance? Create a safe space to discuss any concerns and seek professional guidance if needed.

9. How can we maintain emotional connection and intimacy outside the bedroom? Share ideas on how to nurture emotional intimacy in your relationship.

10. What are some new experiences or activities you'd like to try together to enhance our sexual relationship? Be open to exploring and experimenting in ways that both partners find exciting and comfortable.

Remember that open and non-judgmental communication is essential in addressing these questions and fostering a healthy and fulfilling sexual relationship.

Chapter 5: Navigating Communication and Conflict Resolution

Communication and conflict resolution are essential pillars of a strong and enduring relationship. Effective communication lays the groundwork for understanding, empathy, and connection, while conflict resolution skills empower couples to overcome challenges and grow together.

In this chapter, we'll delve into the intricacies of communication, exploring how to express feelings, needs, and desires openly and honestly. We'll also uncover the art of resolving conflicts, finding common ground, and strengthening the bond between partners. Whether you're a newlywed or have been married for years, mastering these skills is key to nurturing a thriving and resilient partnership.

Conflict Resolution and Mutual Agreement

When it comes to resolving conflicts and reaching mutually agreeable choices, a helpful technique is to visualize two concentric circles. The inner circle represents what is non-negotiable and cannot be compromised, while the outer circle encompasses areas that are negotiable and open to compromise.

During conflicts or disagreements, identifying the nature of the issue and categorizing it within these circles can provide clarity. For negotiable matters, couples can explore various solutions and accommodate each other's preferences. For non-negotiable issues, it's essential to respect each other's boundaries and make decisions accordingly, even if it involves discussing the matter with family members.

Effective Conflict Resolution

In the journey of marriage, conflicts are inevitable, but how couples handle them is crucial. Here are some do's and don'ts for resolving conflicts and maintaining a healthy relationship:

Do's:

- Approach conflicts with the intention of finding solutions, not assigning blame.

- Communicate openly and honestly, expressing your feelings and concerns.

- Use relaxation techniques like deep breathing to calm down during heated moments.

- Give each other space when needed and respect personal boundaries.

- Offer the benefit of the doubt and avoid making assumptions.

- Keep past arguments separate from current conflicts.

- Practice empathy and active listening to truly understand each other.

- Maintain a sense of humour and find opportunities for laughter.

Don'ts:

- Assassinate each other's character or engage in personal attacks.

- Resort to physical aggression or the silent treatment.

- Revisit old fights in new arguments.

- Overgeneralize or make sweeping statements.

- Threaten divorce or use fear tactics as a means of control.

- Involve others, such as family members or colleagues, in your disputes.

- Demean or belittle each other in any way.

- Engage in serious discussions when consumed by anger.

- Take words spoken in anger to heart when making important decisions.

- Be excessively clingy or overly suspicious of your partner.

- Use vulnerabilities or past pain points as weapons.

- Intentionally hurt each other where it hurts the most.

- Bring conflicts into the workplace or involve co-workers.

- Neglect the impact of your disagreements on neighbours.

- Argue in front of children or speak negatively about each other in their presence.

Remember, as couples grow older together, they also grow wiser. Providing each other with chances for growth, understanding, and love is the key to building a marriage that stands the test of time. By following these guidelines, couples can navigate the challenges of life together while preserving the love and respect that brought them together in the first place.

Utilising Non-Violent Communication (NVC) for Couples

Effective communication and conflict resolution are vital in maintaining a healthy and harmonious relationship. The Non-Violent Communication (NVC) framework, developed by Marshall Rosenberg, provides couples with valuable tools for addressing conflicts and nurturing understanding. NVC promotes open and empathetic dialogue, facilitating conflict resolution without causing harm to the relationship.

Applying NVC for expressing amicably

It's entirely natural for couples to encounter differences and have requests, whether those requests are related to changes in behaviour or seeking support. However, the way these requests are communicated can significantly impact the outcome of such conversations.

When communication takes on an accusatory tone or style, it can often be off-putting and lead to defensiveness, resistance to change requests, or even dismissal of the issue altogether.

Observation: In effectively applying the Non-Violent Communication (NVC) framework within a relationship, it's imperative to initiate the process with clear, impartial, and non-judgmental observations regarding the situation or issue at hand.

Avoid language that demeans, critiques, or insults your partner. Steer clear of making allegations or judgments about their character. For example, rather than saying, "You never help with the housework," you can neutrally state, "I've noticed that household chores have been challenging for both of us."

This approach fosters an environment of safe and respectful communication, which is essential for conflict resolution and gaining a deeper understanding of each other's perspectives and needs.

Feelings: By openly sharing how a situation or issue makes you feel, you enable your partner to gain a better understanding of your emotional state.

This sharing of emotions should eschew blame, judgment, or accusations. It's about genuinely conveying your emotional responses to a specific circumstance. For instance, instead of accusing, "You never help with household chores," you can express your feelings by stating, "I feel overwhelmed and stressed when there's a lot of housework to do."

Identifying Unmet Needs: Simultaneously, it's vital to express the underlying needs that are not currently being met in that situation. This step elucidates your specific requirements or desires, which may not be immediately apparent to your partner.

These needs can encompass various aspects such as support, understanding, comfort, or the creation of a conducive living environment. To illustrate, alongside your feelings, you can articulate your needs by saying, "I need to have a clean and organized living space."

Requests: Make explicit and precise requests for actions that can help fulfil those needs. Instead of issuing vague directives such as, "You should do more around the house," you can propose a collaborative approach by stating, "Could we discuss a fair division of household chores so that both of us feel supported, and our home remains comfortable?"

The combined expression of feelings and needs, as promoted by NVC, exerts a profound impact on communication within a relationship.

It redirects the focus away from blame or accusations, emphasizing shared comprehension of emotions and needs.

This approach not only mitigates defensive reactions but also cultivates empathy and cooperation between partners. It fosters constructive and empathetic conversations, empowering both individuals to collaborate in finding solutions and effectively meeting each other's needs.

Freedom to say NO to requests:

It's important to remember that just because a request is framed within the NVC framework, it doesn't mean that the partner has no power to say no. In any healthy and respectful relationship, both partners should be prepared to hear and respect each other's boundaries. Always be ready to listen empathetically to what your partner is trying to communicate and strive for a win-win situation where both feel heard, valued, respected, and supported.

Expressing for Change of Behaviour:

1. **Observation**: "I've noticed that we often argue about household chores."

   Feelings: "This makes me feel frustrated and overwhelmed."

   Needs: "I really need a more balanced division of responsibilities at home."

   Request: "Could we discuss and come up with a plan that ensures we both share these tasks more equitably?"

2. **Observation**: "I've observed that we spend less quality time together."

   Feelings: "I feel lonely and disconnected."

   Needs: "I have a need for emotional closeness and intimacy."

Request: "Can we schedule some dedicated time for us to reconnect and strengthen our bond?"

3. **Observation**: "I've seen that we often argue when discussing finances."

Feelings: "This causes me anxiety and stress."

Needs: "I need financial stability and transparency in our relationship."

Request: "Could we set up regular meetings to go over our finances and make joint decisions together?"

Empathetic Listening and Support

Conversations and disagreements are part of any romantic relationships. However, it's not uncommon for what one partner says to be misconstrued or taken in an unintended, often demeaning, way by the other.

This misinterpretation can set off a chain reaction, with one partner overreacting, the other retreating in silence out of fear of escalation, or both compromising to the point of feeling stifled. Over time, these misunderstandings and unspoken tensions can result in a disconnection that erodes the foundation of the relationship.

To navigate these conversational pitfalls and build deeper connections, one can turn to the empathetic listening framework within Non-Violent Communication (NVC). This compassionate approach encourages couples to engage in dialogues that promote understanding and connection while minimizing the potential for defensiveness, judgment, and misunderstanding.

Observation: Empathetic listening starts with paying meticulous attention to your partner's words and non-verbal cues, all while refraining from interrupting or passing judgments. For instance, if your partner vents frustration about their work, take note of their body language, tone of voice, and words to accurately discern their emotions. The goal is to truly understand what they are expressing beyond the surface.

Feelings: Next, it's essential to acknowledge your partner's emotions and let them know that you comprehend what they're experiencing. You might gently reflect, "It sounds like you're feeling overwhelmed at work. Is that an accurate reflection?" This approach demonstrates your sensitivity to their emotional state, fostering a deeper connection.

Needs: Empathetic listening involves probing to identify the underlying needs your partner is trying to convey. If they mention feeling unsupported in their work, it could signify a need for recognition, assistance, or something else entirely. By digging beneath the surface, you can better grasp the root of their emotions.

Requests: Finally, inquire if there's anything specific your partner requires from you to address their needs. For example, you can kindly ask, "Is there a way I can support you during this challenging time at work?" This step underscores your commitment to providing the support and understanding they need.

Empathetic listening also entails steering clear of accusatory language, belittling remarks, judgment, and intolerance. It promotes an environment where both partners feel heard, respected, and valued, paving the way for more profound connections and effective conflict resolution within the relationship.

 By embracing the principles of NVC, couples can build stronger, more empathetic bonds and navigate the inevitable challenges of partnership with grace and understanding.

Here are some examples of how couples can use Non-Violent Communication (NVC) for empathetic listening to each other.

Examples of Empathetic Listening and Responding:

1. **Observation**: "I've noticed you seem upset after our conversations about chores."

Feelings: "Are you feeling overwhelmed or frustrated about the division of household tasks?"

Needs: "It's important for me to understand your perspective and address any concerns you have."

Response: "I'm here to listen and work together to find a solution that works for both of us."

2. **Observation**: "I see that you've been distant lately."

Feelings: "Are you feeling disconnected or unhappy with our relationship?"

Needs: "I want to ensure that we both feel emotionally fulfilled and close."

Response: "I'm here to listen and understand what's been on your mind. How can we work together to improve our connection?"

3. **Observation**: "I've noticed you appear stressed when we discuss money."

Feelings: "Is this causing you anxiety or worry about our financial situation?"

Needs: "I value financial stability and our ability to make decisions together."

Response: "I'm here to listen to your concerns and work on a plan that addresses both of our needs and priorities."

Navigating Conflict: The Power of a Code Word

In the unpredictable journey of life as a couple, there may come times when things take an unexpected turn. Heated arguments can erupt, emotions run high, and the presence of others can sometimes escalate the tension rather than diffuse it. In these challenging moments, things can spiral into irreparable emotional and relational damage.

During these intense exchanges, when it feels like conversations are veering toward character assassination or escalating into a distressing and violent atmosphere, introducing a "code word" or a signal like "RED" can be an invaluable strategy.

This straightforward yet potent tool acts as a lifeline, prompting both partners to pause, step back, and allow emotions to cool before resuming the discussion.

When tensions are at their peak, the mere utterance of the code word becomes a lifeline, signalling the need for both partners to grant each other space and time.

It serves as a protective shield, shielding against harmful or fruitless exchanges and aligning with the crucial principle of managing intense emotions.

By embracing this approach, couples can craft a safer space for communication and conflict resolution, effectively safeguarding their emotional well-being and the resilience of their relationship.

In the midst of life's unpredictable twists and turns, the code word emerges as a beacon of hope, guiding partners back to a place of understanding and harmony.

Here's how you can introduce and use the code word effectively in your conflict resolution:

1. **Agree on the Code Word**: Sit down with your partner and choose a code word or signal that you both agree upon. Make sure it's something easy to remember and not likely to cause additional tension.

2. **Use the Code Word Responsibly**: When you find yourselves in a heated argument and feel that emotions are escalating beyond a productive level, either partner can

calmly say the code word. This signals to both of you that it's time to pause the discussion.

3. **Pause and Reflect:** Upon hearing the code word, both partners should take a break from the argument. Leave the immediate environment if necessary, practice relaxation techniques like deep breathing, or engage in activities that help you calm down.

4. **Respect the Break**: During the break, it's essential to respect each other's need for space. Avoid dwelling on the argument or harbouring resentment during this time. Instead, focus on regaining emotional balance.

5. **Return to the Discussion**: Once you both feel calmer and more collected, return to the conversation with a commitment to using healthy communication techniques. Consider using "I-statements" to express your feelings and needs, as discussed earlier.

6. **Resolve the Conflict**: With a cooler head and improved emotional regulation, you can work together to find constructive solutions to the issue at hand. Remember to prioritize empathy, active listening, and finding common ground.

The use of a code word can be an effective tool for promoting self-awareness, emotional regulation, more respectful communication and healthy conflict resolution within a relationship.

Activity: Figuring your code word

Here are some questions that couples can explore when implementing a code word or signal in their relationship:

1. What Should the Code Word Be?

- Have an open discussion about what the code word or signal should be. It should be something easy to remember and not likely to cause further tension. Consider words or phrases that hold personal significance to both of you.

2. When Should We Use the Code Word?

- Define the situations or contexts in which the code word can be used. Is it only for heated arguments, or can it be used in other scenarios, such as when one partner feels overwhelmed or needs a break from a conversation?

3. What Does the Code Word Signify?

- Clarify the meaning behind the code word. When one of you says it, what does it represent? Is it a signal to pause the conversation, take a break, or shift to a more constructive and calm approach?

4. How Long Should the Break Be?

- Discuss the duration of the break when the code word is used. Should you both agree on a specific time frame, or should it be flexible based on when you feel ready to resume the conversation?

5. What Should We Do During the Break?

- Explore activities or techniques that can help you both cool down and regain emotional balance during the break. Should you engage in deep breathing, go for a walk, or practice relaxation exercises?

6. How Can We Ensure a Respectful Break?

- Emphasise the importance of respecting each other's need for space during the break. Discuss how to avoid harbouring resentment or ruminating on the argument while taking time apart.

7. How Will We Return to the Discussion?

- Determine how you'll signal that you're ready to resume the conversation after the break. Should you both agree to initiate the discussion, or is there another agreed-upon signal to use?

8. What Communication Techniques Will We Use After the Break?

- Talk about the communication strategies you'll employ when you return to the discussion. Consider using "I-statements" to express your feelings and needs, and discuss how you can actively listen to each other.

9. What Is the Ultimate Goal of Using the Code Word?

- Reflect on the purpose of implementing the code word. Is it to prevent hurtful arguments, promote healthier communication, or enhance overall relationship satisfaction?

10. How Will We Evaluate Its Effectiveness?

- Establish a method for assessing whether the code word is achieving its intended goals. Discuss how you'll provide feedback and make any necessary adjustments to improve its effectiveness.

These questions can help couples create a clear and mutually agreed-upon plan for using a code word. Its Important for both partners to feel comfortable and empowered in utilising this tool to enhance conflict resolution and maintain a healthy relationship.

Reconnecting After Conflict: Navigating Initiations and Rebuilding Bonds

Every couple experiences heated arguments or disagreements from time to time. It's a natural part of any relationship. However, what truly matters is how couples navigate the aftermath of these conflicts. Who should initiate the conversation to mend the broken bond, and what rituals can enhance the connection that may have been strained by the disagreement?

Initiating Post-Conflict Conversations

After a heated argument, the question of who should initiate the conversation often arises. In reality, there isn't a one-size-fits-all answer to this. It's more about the willingness to reconnect and heal the emotional wounds.

One partner may often find themselves taking the initiative to apologize or make attempts to rebuild the relationship after a disagreement. They understand the value of open communication and are eager to resolve the conflict rather than allowing it to fester. This proactive approach can be incredibly beneficial for the relationship, as it demonstrates a commitment to growth and understanding.

On the flip side, there are situations where one partner may feel guilty or recognize that they were at fault in the argument. In such cases, they might hesitate to make the first move. The fear of rejection or judgment can lead them to hide or refrain from initiating a conversation. It's crucial for both partners to recognize that it's okay to acknowledge one's mistakes and express the desire to make amends.

Rebuilding Bonds

To enhance the connection that may have been strained by a disagreement, couples can establish rituals or practices that promote reconciliation and emotional healing. These rituals can be unique to each couple, but here are some ideas:

1. **Quality Time**: Spend dedicated quality time together without distractions. This could involve a leisurely walk, a cosy dinner, or simply sitting down to talk and listen to each other.

2. **Reaffirmation of Love**: Express your love and appreciation for each other verbally. Reaffirm your commitment to the relationship.

3. **Apology and Forgiveness**: If an apology is necessary, make it sincere and heartfelt. Similarly, practice forgiveness as a means of letting go of the hurt and moving forward

4. **Affection**: Physical touch, such as hugging, holding hands, or cuddling, can convey care and affection without words.

5. **Shared Activities**: Engage in activities you both enjoy, whether it's a hobby, watching a favourite show, or playing a game together.

6. **Communication**: Use "I-statements" to express your feelings and perspective on the argument, fostering understanding and empathy.

Addressing Silent Treatment and Protracted Conflicts

The silent treatment, where one partner withdraws and stops communicating as a way to express contempt or hurt, should be addressed promptly. It's essential for couples not to let conflicts go unresolved beyond a night or a day at most. Open communication is key to resolving issues.

If one partner consistently employs the silent treatment as a means of coping with conflict, it's vital for both partners to engage in a candid conversation about its impact on the relationship.

In contrast, when one partner habitually initiates conversations to diffuse conflicts, their efforts should be

appreciated and reciprocated. Acknowledging their proactive approach can foster a sense of teamwork and mutual respect.

Acknowledging Efforts and Shared Responsibility

In the process of reconnecting after a conflict, it's essential to recognise that it takes effort from both partners. When one person consistently makes repeated attempts to initiate conversations or rebuild the relationship, regardless of who is at fault, their efforts should be acknowledged and appreciated.

Empowering each other to take the lead in resolving conflicts and nurturing the relationship is a shared responsibility. It cannot be ignored or taken for granted. Both partners need to actively participate in these efforts to create a balanced and healthy relationship dynamic.

 Feeling wanted, cared for, and valued should be a mutual experience in the relationship. It's not about one partner always giving more while the other consistently receives. Instead, it's about both partners reciprocating gestures of love, understanding, and forgiveness.

By actively participating in post-conflict conversations, offering forgiveness, and appreciating each other's efforts, couples can foster a sense of equality and mutual support in their relationship.

In essence, post-conflict reconnection and rebuilding bonds require a combination of proactive communication, understanding, and a willingness to heal.

Both partners play a role in this process, and it's through these efforts that couples can emerge from conflicts stronger and more connected than before. is this okay

Handling difficult relations in marriage

Marriage is more than the union of two individuals; it signifies the merging of two families. Regardless of shared backgrounds or diverse sects, families often possess distinct perspectives. While the previous discussions offer guidance for couples navigating differences, there may still be challenges.

Despite your best efforts, certain differences may persist. In such instances, effective communication plays a vital role. When faced with different viewpoints, initiate a discussion with your partner to establish a unified stance. Engaging in open dialogue about your unified stance with family, can often bridge some of these differences.

In addition, there may be other areas where, as a couple, you aim to understand the emotions, motivations, and sentiments behind differing beliefs, rituals, or viewpoints, especially when dealing with challenging family members or individuals. It's natural for them to have unique backgrounds, experiences, and beliefs that have shaped their viewpoints.

While you respect the differences, you can always define and communicate clearly what you can and cannot compromise on. You can approach these discussions with empathy, patience, and a willingness to find common ground. This includes personal space, traditions, individual choices, career preferences, child rearing etc.

Finding common ground with family members on various aspects is beneficial. When faced with substantial differences, appreciating diversity fosters an open environment within the family. This openness encourages consideration of your viewpoint and promotes a spirit of compromise.

While navigating through these complex yet sensitive family dynamics, it's important to stay true to yourself. Instead of seeking constant approval, aim for authenticity. Avoid placing yourself on a pedestal or idolizing others blindly. Everyone, including you, has their highs and lows, so embrace imperfections and make peace with the reality that you can't please everyone. This mindset fosters self-acceptance and prevents exhaustion and burnout.

Resist the temptation to undermine your own worth or compromise your values for the sake of pleasing others. Establish firm boundaries and prioritize your well-being, ensuring that your actions align with your authentic self.

Recognise the uniqueness of each individual, including yourself, within the family structure. Uphold your individuality while navigating familial expectations, fostering an environment that respects diverse perspectives.

Striking a balance between familial harmony and personal fulfilment is essential. While compromise is a part of any relationship, ensure that it doesn't come at the cost of losing your sense of self. Healthy relationships involve mutual understanding and respect for individual identities.

Prioritise valuing yourself and expressing your viewpoint to your family or the difficult member. It's common for others to influence you when you're unclear, potentially leading you away from your values and interests. Therefore, it's crucial to maintain a sense of self-worth and confidence in your collective stance on every differing aspect or potential area of strain.

By embracing these principles, you empower yourself to navigate family dynamics with authenticity and resilience. This approach fosters a harmonious environment where both family unity and personal identity coexist, creating a space where you can contribute to and thrive within the family.

There's no bond quite like that of family. When you come together, bridging differences, you create a space akin to heaven. Your home transforms into a safety net and support system, where concerns, challenges, stress, and worries can be openly discussed. It becomes a conducive environment that fosters unity and mutual assistance.

As you work towards cultivating a healthy immediate family, including your parents and in-laws, it's essential to prioritise the interests of both partners. This involves approaching differences with respect, tolerance, empathy, and open-mindedness.

Be willing to compromise when necessary, firmly asserting your stance on certain matters. Implement healthy communication and conflict resolution strategies to maintain harmony within your family.

Navigating Partner-Parent Dynamics for Relationship Harmony

Dealing with a situation where your partner seems more aligned with their parents than with you can be challenging. Here are some steps you might consider:

1. **Open Communication:** Express your feelings to your partner in a calm and non-confrontational manner. Share your concerns and let them know how their actions are affecting you. Choose a time when you can have an uninterrupted and focused conversation.

2. **Seek Understanding:** Try to understand your partner's perspective. It's possible that they may not be fully aware of how their actions are impacting you. Encourage them to share their feelings and thoughts about their relationship with their parents.

3. **Establish Boundaries:** Discuss and set healthy boundaries that work for both of you. It's crucial to find a balance between maintaining a connection with parents and prioritising your relationship. Clearly define the roles and expectations in your relationship.

4. **Couples Counselling:** If the issue persists and becomes a source of dissatisfaction, consider seeking the help of a couples counsellor. A professional can provide guidance and facilitate discussions to improve understanding and communication between you and your partner.

5. **Build a Support System:** Cultivate a support system outside of your relationship. This could include friends, family, or a therapist. Having people to talk to and share your feelings with can provide additional perspectives and emotional support.

6. **Focus on Self-Care**: Take care of your own well-being. Ensure that you are engaging in activities that bring you joy and fulfilment. This can help you maintain a sense of self-worth and independence.

7. **Evaluate Long-Term Goals**: Reflect on your long-term goals and priorities in the relationship. Consider whether both partners are willing to make adjustments for the sake of mutual happiness and fulfilment. If needed, revisit and revise your shared goals.

Chapter 6: Growth, Trust, and Thriving Relationships

In the journey of marriage, nurturing a relationship that thrives and stands the test of time requires deliberate efforts in various domains. In this section, we'll delve into the vital role of encouraging each other's aspirations and providing unwavering support in the pursuit of personal goals.

We'll also discuss the importance of trust-building, transparency, and open communication in fortifying the bonds of love. By embracing growth and trust as cornerstones of their relationship, couples can forge a path towards lasting happiness and mutual fulfilment.

Supporting Your Partner's Growth

In a healthy and thriving relationship, it's crucial to strike a balance between providing guidance and trusting your partner's capabilities.

While it's natural to offer advice and support when your partner faces challenges, it's equally important to recognize when to step back and have confidence in their ability to navigate difficulties.

Repeatedly giving advice may unintentionally convey a lack of trust in their capabilities. Trust is a cornerstone of a strong relationship, and demonstrating your belief in your partner's competence can be empowering and affirming.

Moreover, a hallmark of a great relationship is genuinely supporting each other in the pursuit of dreams and goals. Celebrating your partner's successes, no matter how small, fosters an environment of encouragement and shared joy.

As your partner's number one cheerleader, you contribute to their motivation and self-esteem. Being genuinely happy for your partner's achievements not only strengthens your bond but also reinforces the idea that you're a team working towards each other's aspirations.

Activity: Explore preferences

Here are some suggested conversations to help partners navigate the balance between providing guidance and trusting each other's capabilities in a relationship:

1. Discussing Communication Styles:

- When one of us is facing a challenge, when do you think is the ideal time for us to discuss day-to-day issues, problems, or anything that might be bothering us?

- If I have something challenging to share or a problem I've faced, how can I sensitively communicate that to you? How do you prefer to receive this kind of information, and what makes you feel supported or empowered in those moments?

- When I need something or want to address an issue, what would be the best way for me to communicate that with you?

2.Setting Boundaries:

- Let's explore when it's appropriate to provide guidance and when trusting each other's judgment is key.

- How can we recognise when to offer tangible or emotional support versus when to listen and allow the other to handle things independently?

- In situations where one of us may have more expertise, how can we communicate effectively, especially if the other might be hesitant to listen or accept advice?

- Are there specific scenarios where you'd prefer more input, or do you feel more comfortable handling certain matters independently?

3. Expressing Trust:

- I value our trust in each other. How can we reassure each other that, even when offering advice, it comes from a place of support and belief in each other's capabilities?

4. Celebrating Successes:

- I want us to be each other's biggest cheerleaders. How can we make sure we celebrate our successes, both big and small, and contribute to each other's motivation and self-esteem?

- How can we celebrate each other's successes, even if they happen at different paces or magnitudes? What are meaningful ways to acknowledge achievements without feelings of jealousy?

- If feelings of jealousy arise, during periods of individual success, how can we openly discuss them without judgment? What strategies can we implement to ensure our relationship remains a source of strength?

5. Discussing Long-Term Goals:

- Let's talk about our individual long-term goals.

- How can we support each other in achieving them while ensuring we maintain trust and independence in our pursuits, even when our paths may differ?

- Are there specific ways you'd like to be supported during times of professional growth?

- Are there shared goals we can establish as a couple?

- How can we work towards accomplishments that benefit both of us and reinforce our unity?

6. Reflecting on Past Experiences:

- Can we share past experiences where advice or trust played a significant role?

- What did we learn from those situations, and how can we apply those lessons to our current relationship?

7. Creating a Support Plan:

- How can we create a support plan that balances offering guidance with trusting each other's capabilities?

- Are there specific phrases or actions that make you feel supported and encouraged?

Navigating Divergent Professional Paths in a Relationship

In the journey of a relationship, partners may find themselves on different trajectories in their professional lives. This divergence can be challenging, especially when one outgrows the other in their career or when circumstances lead to varied levels of professional engagement.

However, with open communication, shared definitions of success, and a commitment to acknowledging each other's contributions, couples can navigate these differences successfully.

During these times, it's important for partners to support each other's success, celebrate achievements collectively, and ensure that both individuals feel valued and empowered on their unique career paths.

Activity: Explore preferences

Supporting a partner's success, especially when there's a significant disparity in professional achievements, requires understanding, empathy, and effective communication.

Here are some ways to approach this:

1. Open Communication:

- Let's discuss our individual career paths and goals openly.

- How can we ensure that both of us feel valued and supported in our respective journeys?

- What expectations or concerns do we have about our roles in and outside of the workplace?

2. Defining Success Together:

  - What does success look like for each of us, and are there shared definitions of success as a couple?

- How can we celebrate achievements, big or small, in a way that feels inclusive and supportive?

3. Acknowledging Contributions:

  - Even if our professional paths differ, how can we acknowledge and appreciate the contributions each of us makes to the family and our overall well-being?

- How can we ensure that neither of us feels diminished or overlooked?

4. Celebrating Jointly:

  - Are there joint celebrations we can plan for both of our successes, regardless of the scale or nature?

- How can we make sure that success for one is a victory for both?

By addressing these questions with communication, partners can navigate differences in career trajectories.

Avoiding Jealousy and Possessiveness

Jealousy and possessiveness can be detrimental to a relationship. Trust is the foundation of a strong partnership, and it's essential to trust your partner's loyalty and commitment. Instead of giving in to jealousy, focus on open communication, understanding, and building a sense of security within the relationship.

Trust is not just about believing that your partner won't betray you but also about knowing that you can openly discuss your feelings and concerns. Healthy relationships are built on mutual respect, transparency, and the freedom for each person to maintain their individuality while being part of a loving partnership.

Activity: Explore preferences

Here are some questions that couples can ask each other to address feelings of jealousy or possessiveness and enhance their sense of security in the relationship:

1. Can we talk openly about our feelings of jealousy or insecurity without judgment?

2. What specific actions or behaviours trigger these feelings for you, and how can we work together to address them?

3. Do you feel that our communication is transparent enough to discuss concerns about opposite-gender friendships or interactions at work?

4. Are there specific boundaries or guidelines that you believe would help alleviate your concerns and make you feel more secure?

5. How can we ensure that we prioritize quality time together to strengthen our connection and prevent feelings of neglect?

6. In what ways can we build trust and reassure each other of our commitment, especially when spending time with others of the opposite gender?

7. Do you feel comfortable expressing your needs for reassurance, and how can I support you in those moments?

8. Are there activities or shared experiences that we can incorporate into our routine to strengthen our bond and reduce feelings of insecurity?

9. Can we establish guidelines for maintaining individuality within the relationship while ensuring that both partners feel valued and secure?

10. How can we work together to foster a sense of trust and security that goes beyond just avoiding jealousy but

actively building a foundation of confidence in our relationship?

Fostering a Thriving Relationship: The Role of Patience, Forgiveness, and Compassion

Relationships are dynamic journeys, filled with moments of joy and challenges alike. It's only natural for couples to encounter differences, have requests for changes in behaviour, or seek support from one another. However, the manner in which we communicate these needs and navigate conflicts can profoundly influence the health and durability of our partnerships.

Patience and Tolerance for Mistakes

Patience, a valuable virtue, stands at the heart of nurturing a thriving relationship. It encompasses the willingness to grant each other time and space for growth, evolution, and adaptation. In the context of couples, patience is closely intertwined with tolerance for mistakes.

Understanding that none of us is perfect and that errors are an inherent part of the journey of love is key. Tolerance for these missteps entails resisting the urge to rush to judgment or become excessively critical when blunders occur.

Instead, it centers on recognising that both partners are works in progress, each learning and growing through shared experiences.

Heartfelt Apologies and Seeking Forgiveness

Inevitably, mistakes will happen, or one partner may unintentionally cause pain. In such moments, the significance of heartfelt apologies and seeking forgiveness cannot be overstated.

A heartfelt apology constitutes a genuine admission of one's mistakes or acknowledgment of the hurt inflicted on a partner. It's a demonstration of remorse and an earnest commitment to rectify the situation.

Seeking forgiveness, conversely, showcases humility and a sincere desire to mend the relationship. It signifies an acceptance of one's capacity for errors and a plea for an opportunity to make amends.

These actions are potent tools for healing and rebuilding trust within a relationship. They foster understanding, empathy, and a shared determination to move forward.

Constructive Feedback vs. Derogatory Remarks

a. **Constructive Feedback:** Providing constructive feedback involves addressing concerns or areas for improvement with kindness and empathy. It concentrates on solutions and personal growth, aiming to bring out the best in each other.

b. **Derogatory Remarks**: Derogatory remarks or criticism, in contrast, can be destructive and hurtful. They target the person rather than the behaviour, leading to defensiveness and emotional pain.

 A healthier approach involves using "I" statements, focusing on the specific behaviour or situation you wish to address, suggesting solutions, and approaching feedback with the intention of supporting your partner's growth and development.

The Essence of Compassion

At the core of all these elements lies compassion—the ability to understand, empathize, and support one another, even in moments of conflict or when confronting our imperfections.

Compassion serves as a constant reminder that both partners are on this journey together, firmly committed to each other's well-being and personal growth.

In conclusion, a thriving relationship is built on the foundational principles of patience, tolerance, heartfelt apologies, forgiveness, expressions of love, and constructive feedback—all bound together by the thread of compassion.

By wholeheartedly embracing these principles, couples can navigate challenges, heal wounds, and cultivate a partnership that not only withstands the test of time but also flourishes, filling the lives of both individuals with enduring joy and fulfilment.

Handling Common Disconnection Concerns

Cultural and interfaith relationships

Cultural and interfaith relationships can be rich and rewarding, but they also come with unique challenges.

Couples from different backgrounds often need to navigate differences in traditions, values, and religious beliefs. It's essential to approach these relationships with an open heart and a willingness to learn from one another.

Activity: Explore preferences

1. How do our cultural backgrounds shape our values, traditions, and expectations in a relationship?

2. What are the most significant cultural or religious differences between us, and how do they impact our daily lives and decision-making?

3. How can we celebrate and honour each other's cultural or religious traditions while maintaining our own identities?

4. Are there specific challenges we've faced in our interfaith or intercultural relationship, and how have we overcome them?

5. What role will our cultural or religious beliefs play in major life decisions, such as marriage, parenting, or end-of-life care?

6. How can we ensure that our families and communities respect and support our relationship, even if it challenges traditional norms?

Long-Distance Relationships

Maintaining a strong and healthy long-distance relationship requires effective communication, trust, and a commitment to staying connected despite the physical distance. It can be challenging, but with the right strategies, long-distance couples can thrive.

Activity: Explore preferences

1. What are our primary goals and expectations for our long-distance relationship?

2. How often should we communicate, and what platforms or methods work best for us?

3. How can we keep the romance alive despite the physical separation?

4. What strategies can we implement to build trust and prevent jealousy or insecurity?

5. Are there specific milestones or goals we want to achieve before closing the distance?

6. How can we manage the financial aspects of a long-distance relationship, such as travel expenses?

Technology and Relationships

Technology has revolutionised the way couples communicate, but it also comes with its share of challenges. Issues like excessive screen time, digital privacy, and the impact of social media can affect relationships.

Activity: Explore preferences

1. How does our use of technology impact our relationship? Are there any concerns or areas for improvement?

2. Do we have boundaries in place for screen time and device use when we're together or apart?

3. How can we ensure that our digital communication enhances our connection rather than detracts from it?

4. Are there social media rules or guidelines we should establish to protect our privacy and maintain trust?

5. Have there been instances where technology caused misunderstandings or conflicts in our relationship, and how can we prevent them in the future?

6. What role does technology play in our intimacy and emotional connection?

Mental Health and Relationships

Mental health is closely intertwined with relationship well-being. Couples need to support each other through mental health challenges and prioritize self-care

Activity: Explore preferences

1. How can we best support each other's mental health and well-being?

2. Are there specific signs or triggers of stress, anxiety, or depression that we should be aware of in each other?

3. What strategies can we implement to manage stress and maintain a healthy work-life balance?

4. When is it appropriate to seek professional help or therapy for individual or relationship issues?

5. How can we ensure that our relationship remains a source of emotional support during challenging times?

6. What role does open communication play in addressing mental health concerns within our relationship?

Infidelity and Trust

Infidelity can be one of the most difficult challenges a couple faces. Rebuilding trust and moving forward after a breach of trust is a complex process.

Activity: Explore preferences

Here are some conversational cues to be made in the process of knowing each other's views about Infidelity.

1. Have we discussed our boundaries and expectations regarding fidelity and trust within our relationship?

2. What would be our approach to rebuilding trust if infidelity were to occur?

3. Are there underlying issues or unmet needs within our relationship that could lead to infidelity, and how can we address them proactively?

4. How can we ensure that both partners feel secure and valued in our relationship?

5. What steps can we take to prevent infidelity and protect the trust we've built?

6. What role does forgiveness play in healing from infidelity, and how can we work towards forgiving and rebuilding?

Rebuilding Trust After Infidelity: Strategies for Healing in a Relationship

Infidelity can pose a significant hurdle for couples who are married or in serious committed relations. It often originates from a lack of emotional connection or satisfaction in the relationship.

Various factors, such as breakdowns in communication, feelings of neglect, unmet emotional or physical needs, and emotional distance, can create conditions that lead one partner to seek emotional connections outside the relationship.

This pursuit of emotional connection may escalate into physical intimacy. Hence, emotional intimacy is a pivotal element in a thriving relationship, and its absence can result in sensations of loneliness or dissatisfaction, potentially paving the way for infidelity.

Recognising the importance of emotional intimacy, couples should actively strive to nurture and sustain a robust emotional connection, even in the aftermath of infidelity. While it can be a painful experience, couples must acknowledge the signs of disconnection in the relationship.

At this juncture, couples are faced with a choice: either commit to rebuilding the emotional connection through honest, mutual communication and trust or succumb to the pain and further distance themselves from each other. Empathy, active listening, and a willingness to understand each other's emotional needs play vital roles in preventing the erosion of emotional intimacy. The Nonviolent Communication (NVC) framework, as discussed in preceding chapters on listening, can be a valuable reference.

It is crucial to delve into the underlying issues that may have played a role in the occurrence of infidelity. Understanding these root causes is essential for addressing deeper problems within the relationship and taking steps to prevent future issues.

Initiating open and honest conversations about infidelity becomes paramount. Sharing feelings, concerns, and expectations openly is a key component of effective communication, serving as the foundation for rebuilding trust.

Rebuilding trust is a gradual process that requires patience and understanding from both partners. Rushing the timeline may hinder the natural progression of healing, emphasizing the need for a shared consensus.

Establishing clear communication and boundaries within the relationship is vital. Both partners should align on expectations, commitments, and future behaviour to ensure they are on the same page moving forward.

Regardless of the agreed-upon terms, incessant reminders, doubts, suspicious monitoring, and passive-aggressive communication can hinder the process. In such situations, forgiveness becomes paramount.

The partner who engaged in infidelity must acknowledge their mistake. Sometimes, individuals struggle with admitting fault due to ego or a constant need to be right. It's crucial to create a non-judgmental space for the other partner to feel safe in committing to seeking forgiveness.

This understanding and commitment to a forgiving environment contribute to the healing process. Initiating open conversations about the impact of cheating can sometimes prompt the other person to lower their defences.

However, it's essential to acknowledge that forgiveness may be a gradual process. It's a mutual journey, and both partners need to actively work towards forgiving each other and releasing any lingering resentment. Recognizing forgiveness as a gift to oneself and the partner fosters healing and paves the way for a renewed and healthier relationship.

Dedicate time and energy to rebuild emotional intimacy by engaging in activities that strengthen your connection—whether it's spending quality time, creating shared experiences, or openly expressing love and appreciation.

Demonstrate commitment to each other, offering support throughout the journey of rebuilding trust. Maintain open communication, discuss feelings, progress, and any concerns that may arise.

Patience is key in this process, as it's natural for mistakes to occur. Investing in these efforts can yield the fruits of a happy and connected marriage, making it a worthwhile endeavour. Isn't that something worth trying?

Aging and Relationships

As couples age together, they face new challenges related to retirement, health, and maintaining emotional closeness. These challenges require open communication and adaptability.

Activity: Explore preferences

1. What are our expectations and plans for retirement, and how do they align with each other's goals and dreams?

2. How can we ensure that we remain emotionally connected and continue to nurture our intimacy as we age?

3. Are there health concerns or potential caregiving responsibilities we need to discuss and plan for?

4. How can we adapt to changes in our physical abilities and maintain an active and fulfilling lifestyle as we grow older?

5. What role will our extended family, including children and grandchildren, play in our lives as we age?

Introduction to Abuse cycle

The abuse cycle is a repeated pattern of behaviour that is common in abusive relationships. It usually consists of several stages, such as tension building, an outburst of abuse, and a period of calm or reconciliation. Understanding this cycle is crucial for recognising and coping with abusive dynamics within relationships. Individuals can disrupt the cycle and work towards better, safer interactions by breaking the silence and getting help.

Domestic abuse and violence often follow a pattern with distinct steps. While variations exist, a common framework includes:

1. Tension Building Phase:

- Minor conflicts and stressors arise, leading to increased tension.

- Communication breakdown and escalating arguments.

- Victims feel the need to tread carefully to avoid triggering explosive reactions.

2. Incident or Explosion Phase:

- The tension peaks, leading to an abusive incident.

- Verbal, emotional, physical, or sexual abuse may occur.

- The abusive partner loses control, leading to violent or aggressive behaviour.

3. Reconciliation or Honeymoon Phase:

- The abuser expresses remorse, apologizes, and may promise it won't happen again.

- The abuser tries to regain the victims trust through gifts, affection, or gestures of kindness.

- The victim may believe the abuse won't happen again.

4. Calm Phase:

  - The relationship appears normal, and there may be no signs of abuse.

  - Both parties may try to move forward.

  - The victim may believe the abuse won't recur, fostering a false sense of security.

5. Building Tension Again:

  - The cycle restarts with the re-emergence of stress and tension.

  - The relationship becomes increasingly volatile.

  - The likelihood of another abusive incident rises.

Understanding these steps empowers individuals to recognize the signs of abuse, seek help, and break free from the cycle. Victims can reach out to support networks, hotlines, or professional services to navigate the complexities of domestic abuse and violence.

Chapter 7: Everyday Practices for Nurturing a Strong Relationship

Building a strong and enduring relationship requires continuous effort and commitment from both partners. While grand gestures and special occasions are essential, it's the small, everyday practices that truly fortify the bond between couples.

Quality Time Together and Combined Rituals

Every day, make an effort to spend quality time with your partner. Whether it's a simple breakfast together, a shared evening walk, or even a heartfelt conversation before bed, these moments foster connection and intimacy.

Additionally, create combined rituals that align with your shared interests. These can be weekly activities like cooking together, going for hikes, or participating in a hobby you both enjoy.

Open and Honest Communication

Honesty and open communication are the cornerstones of trust. Make it a habit to communicate openly every day, sharing your thoughts, feelings, and concerns with your partner. Listen actively and without judgment to what your partner has to say. Share your daily life accomplishments and problems, and seek resolutions together as a team.

Acts of Love in Their Language

Express your love and commitment daily in a way that resonates with your partner's primary love language. Small acts of kindness, like a loving text message, a surprise cup of coffee, or a warm hug, go a long way in reaffirming your affection for each other.

Using your partner's love language ensures that they feel loved, cherished, and adored in a way that truly speaks to their heart.

Patience and Forgiveness

Embrace the qualities of patience and forgiveness in your daily interactions. Recognize that both you and your partner are works in progress, capable of making mistakes and learning from them.

When disagreements or missteps occur, practice patience by giving each other the time and understanding to grow. Extend forgiveness as a powerful tool for healing and rebuilding trust within your relationship.

Avoid dwelling on past errors or seeking revenge, and instead, focus on moving forward together with a spirit of humility and acceptance. Holding onto past hurts can only hinder the growth and freedom of your hearts and relationship.

Humility

Embrace humility in your daily interactions. Acknowledge your own imperfections and be willing to apologize when you're wrong. Equally important, be quick to forgive when your partner makes mistakes.

 Recognize that we all have weaknesses, and relationships have a way of revealing these faults. A healthy marriage is built on the foundation of humility, where both partners can admit their imperfections and seek forgiveness when needed.

Avoid the trap of feeling superior to your partner, as it can lead to resentment and hinder the progress of your relationship. Instead, practice humility by recognizing your partner's strengths and attributes, fostering an environment of mutual respect and growth.

Trust and Honesty

Cultivate trust through daily acts of honesty and transparency. Trust is the bedrock on which a strong relationship is constructed. Honesty and trust are the cornerstones of a healthy marriage.

However, unlike many other aspects of a relationship that can be developed in an instant, trust is something that evolves over time. Trust is the result of consistently being truthful and dependable in all your interactions.

It's not something that can be rushed; rather, it's nurtured over weeks, months, and years of consistently being true to your word and living up to your commitments. Building and maintaining trust is an ongoing effort, so start now.

If trust in your relationship has been compromised, be prepared to put in extra effort to rebuild it, as it will require time and dedication.

Selflessness

Prioritise your partner's happiness and needs occasionally through acts of kindness, like cooking their favourite meal or helping with chores.

In contrast, selfishness can underlie many marital issues, leading to discord. A selfish person is often focused on their desires, lacks patience, and struggles as a partner. In a successful marriage, generosity, sharing, and support for each other's aspirations are essential.

Sexual Faithfulness

Sexual faithfulness in marriage extends beyond our physical bodies to our thoughts, emotions, and soul. Engaging in sexual fantasies about others or sharing emotional intimacy with someone else undermines our faithfulness to our spouse.

It requires daily self-discipline and a clear understanding of the consequences. Guard your sexuality, committing it entirely to your spouse, and prioritize trust and intimacy in your relationship by honouring this commitment every day."

Gratitude and Positive Strokes

Make it a daily practice to express gratitude for your partner's presence in your life. Take time to appreciate the small gestures and actions they do for you.

 Never take their love and support for granted. In addition to gratitude, offer daily positive strokes, such as compliments and words of affirmation, to uplift your partner's spirit and reinforce the love between you.

Acknowledging and expressing gratitude, along with providing positive strokes, fosters a deeper sense of connection and appreciation in your relationship. It reminds both partners of the value and importance you hold for each other, strengthening the bond you share.

Compassion

Compassion is the cornerstone of a thriving relationship, and it should be woven into your everyday interactions. Listen actively, empathise with your partner's perspective, offer tangible support in times of need, show affection, be patient and resolve conflicts kindly.

 By practicing these daily acts of compassion, you create a relationship that flourishes on a foundation of understanding, support, and love, even in the face of challenges.

Remember that nurturing a strong relationship is an ongoing journey. These everyday practices create a foundation of love, trust, and mutual respect. By incorporating them into your daily life, you not only strengthen your bond but also ensure that your relationship continues to thrive and bring joy to both individuals.

Chapter 8: Beyond Boundaries: Navigating Love and Relationships with Open Hearts

Love has no boundaries. This guide promotes the idea that love has no gender or borders and is a fundamental right for everyone, regardless of sexual orientation. While much of the information in the preceding chapters applies to all couples, here are a few additional points to consider.

Understanding Challenges in LGBTQ+ Relationships

While LGBTQ+ relationships share many similarities with other types of relationships, they also face distinct problems. It is critical to discuss these issues openly, acknowledging the resilience and power that come from managing cultural expectations and changing norms.

Celebrating Love Unapologetically:

In a world where legal recognition varies, celebrate your love without reservation. Recognise that the essence of your relationship is defined by the sincerity of your connection, not by external validations.

Communication Excellence:

Any effective partnership is built on open communication. Effective communication is even more important in LGBTQ+ partnerships, where shared experiences and individual identities intersect. Discussing feelings, expectations, and dreams can help you understand and connect with one another.

Individual Identity Support:

In LGBTQ+ relationships, partners often bring a rich set of identities. It is important to support and celebrate these unique Identities within the relationship. Acknowledge the growth that comes from embracing personal journeys and the positive impact it can have on the overall relationship.

Navigating Shared Spaces:

Explore the dynamics of shared spaces in LGBTQ+ relationships. From cohabitation to having a safe and affirming home, understand the nuances that contribute to building a supporting environment where both partners feel valued, respected, and loved.

Creating Your Own Traditions:

Create and embrace your own traditions in the absence of legal frameworks. Create a foundation that reflects your individual path, values, and common experiences.

Building Supportive Networks:

Surround yourself with friends, family, and communities who will support you. Seek out allies who respect and acknowledge the importance of your relationship, contributing to a positive and affirming environment.

Embracing Individuality:

Recognise and appreciate each other's uniqueness inside the relationship. Cultivating a strong sense of self and mutual support is critical in a world that might not fully understand or approve of your union.

Dealing with External Pressures and Fostering Resilience

LGBTQ+ couples are frequently subjected to external pressures and discrimination. Building resilience is essential for navigating these difficulties while maintaining a solid and supportive relationship.

Strengthening Bond Amidst Prejudices:

External prejudices might be intimidating, but using them to strengthen your bond can be empowering. Together, face these challenges with resilience and use them as opportunities for growth.

Community Engagement:

Engaging with the LGBTQ+ community provides a network of support and understanding. Participate in community events, advocacy, and outreach efforts to build resilience and share experiences.

Educating Allies:

Take the initiative to educate friends, family, and colleagues about LGBTQ+ issues. By fostering understanding and awareness, you contribute to creating an environment that is more accepting and supportive.

Importance of Consent in Intimacy:

Emphasise the importance of consent in intimate relationships. Open communication about desires, boundaries, and consent is not only crucial for a healthy sexual relationship but also contributes to a sense of security and trust within the partnership.

Family Dynamics and Acceptance:

Addressing family dynamics and seeking acceptance may take time. Provide resources to help family members understand LGBTQ+ experiences and engage in open conversations to foster understanding.

Promoting Inclusivity Beyond LGBTQ+:

Advocate for inclusion not only within the LGBTQ+ community but also outside of it. Encourage individuals of all sexual orientations and gender identities to be open-minded, accepting, and understanding.

Intersectionality Awareness:

Acknowledge the intersecting identities within the LGBTQ+ community. Understand the specific problems that people with intersecting identities face and work towards creating an inclusive and safe environment for all.

Emotional & physical Well-being:

Prioritise each other's emotional and physical well-being. Establish open communication to discuss feelings, concerns, and experiences. Emotional protection involves creating a safe and supportive environment where both partners can express themselves freely without fear of judgment. Exercise every day, even if it is only for 30 minutes.

Safe Sex Education:

Prioritise ongoing education about safe sex practices specific to LGBTQ+ individuals. Stay informed about preventive measures, including the use of barrier methods such as condoms, regular testing for sexually transmitted infections (STIs), and vaccination options.

A Grateful Farewell

If you've reached this page, thank you for investing time in this extensive guide. Drawing from my 15 years of experience as a relationship expert, I aimed to cover diverse facets to enhance emotional compatibility in couples. I hope you shall put the theory into practise with the aid of conversation cues provided and take steps towards creating your own happily ever after.

My mission is to safeguard the sanctity of marriages, fostering harmonious, joyful, and peaceful lives for couples and families alike.

I invite you to join hands with me in sharing this mission with those around you. Kindly consider rating this book, share it with those in your life, and contribute to helping them shape their own happily ever after. Your support is invaluable in spreading the essence of enduring love and connection.

May your journey be filled with love, understanding, and enduring happiness.

Love

Teju

THE END